PREPARING THE BRIDE OF CHRIST

ALEX DELPERCIO

WESTBOW®
PRESS
A DIVISION OF THOMAS NELSON
& ZONDERVAN

Scripture taken from the New King James Version. Copyright 1979, 1980, 1982 by Thomas Nelson, inc. Used by permission. All rights reserved.

Scripture taken from the King James Version of the Bible.

Scriptures taken from the Holy Bible, New International Version®, NIV®. Copyright © 1973, 1978, 1984, 2011 by Biblica, Inc.™ Used by permission of Zondervan. All rights reserved worldwide. www.zondervan.com The "NIV" and "New International Version" are trademarks registered in the United States Patent and Trademark Office by Biblica, Inc.™ All rights reserved.

Scripture taken from the *Amplified Bible*, Copyright © 1954, 1958, 1962, 1964, 1965, 1987 by The Lockman Foundation. Used by permission.

WestBow Press books may be ordered through booksellers or by contacting:

WestBow Press
A Division of Thomas Nelson & Zondervan
1663 Liberty Drive
Bloomington, IN 47403
www.westbowpress.com
1 (866) 928-1240

Because of the dynamic nature of the Internet, any web addresses or links contained in this book may have changed since publication and may no longer be valid. The views expressed in this work are solely those of the author and do not necessarily reflect the views of the publisher, and the publisher hereby disclaims any responsibility for them.

Any people depicted in stock imagery provided by Thinkstock are models, and such images are being used for illustrative purposes only. Certain stock imagery © Thinkstock.

ISBN: 978-1-4908-2448-2 (sc)
ISBN: 978-1-4908-2449-9 (hc)
ISBN: 978-1-4908-2447-5 (e)

Library of Congress Control Number: 2014901666

Printed in the United States of America.

WestBow Press rev. date: 7/23/2014

To my loving and faithful wife, Linda, who, through her support, has been a helper and has enabled me to give my attention to the study and the ministry of the Word of God.

CONTENTS

FOREWORD

Alex Delpercio has been a good friend of mine for thirty-three years. We have fellowshipped together, laughed and cried together, rock climbed together, and ministered together. He has joined me several times in my ministry to the pastors of Central America. I greatly respect him as a true servant of the Lord who lives out the life of which he speaks. He is also an excellent and well-respected Bible teacher, having now taught at Cornerstone Bible Center for twenty-six years, where he presently serves as the director of the school as well. He answered many of my own questions about the Bible when we first met (I was a new believer), and he loves to share God's wisdom with those who have hungry hearts. Al has a wonderful grasp of the Word of God and ably communicates not just the facts about God but also His ways. He has great insight into the deeper walk with God, which transcends the outward events and circumstances of life.

In his book *Preparing the Bride of Christ*, he presents a much-needed challenge to all of us who say we are Christians to surrender wholeheartedly to the dealings of God in our lives. He helps us to understand that the Lord's purpose and heart in these dealings is to build us up so that we would be made ready for the coming marriage supper of the Lamb and His bride. Are we preparing ourselves? Do we understand what that entails? Many of us do not.

We've all heard of a "diamond in the rough." But not many of us have ever seen one. At that stage a diamond is not much to look at. Yet after being carefully cut, lopped, and polished, a stunning jewel of great value is revealed, able to reflect light and even break it up into the beautiful colors of the rainbow. When we come to the Lord, we are like that diamond in the rough. Perhaps not much to look at on the outside, but on the inside we are a sparkling new creation waiting to be revealed. The world often cannot see the beauty of the new creation within until much cutting, lopping, and polishing takes place. These are the dealings of God in the believer, which He calls our sanctification (1 Thessalonians 4:3). It is the revelation of His own character, and that is something God desires for all of His children.

Unfortunately, some of us do not submit to the process, and so we are not conformed to His image. Paul once addressed the Galatians, "My little children, of whom I travail in birth again until Christ be formed in you" (Galatians 4:19). And today Biblical illiteracy, spiritual apathy, and compromise are common. So I am so thankful for *Preparing the Bride of Christ*. It will clearly and comprehensively take you through the various aspects of the sanctification process. You will be challenged and moved to respond as you read it. You will see your high calling as the bride and understand the path on which you need to walk in order to fulfill that calling. May we all rise to accept the challenge, and together may we become the brilliant, multifaceted diamond that reflects Jesus' light and glory to all creation—the bride of Christ.

Eric J. Fox
Missionary to the pastors of Central America
School of Christ Seminars

###

I have known Alex Delpercio since 1995, when he was one of my Bible school teachers. It was easily recognized that he was a man in whom the Lord had gifted to be a teacher. I have not personally met anyone who has been as dedicated or given as much priority to the study of God's Word. Over the years the Lord has blessed hundreds if not thousands in the United States and abroad through his teaching ministry.

It has been my experience in my years being a Christian that the purity of the gospel of Christ is a rare thing to be found in the world today. Unfortunately there is no shortage of denominations, religions, doctrines, and opinions on the Word of God. It seems that there is always a new spin being put on the gospel to make it more palatable to the individual. The truth is the natural man does not receive the things of the Spirit of God because they are foolishness to Him (1 Corinthians 2:14)! This subjective approach to the preaching, teaching, and even hearing of the gospel has left the church and, more importantly, the people of God in a state quite different from what the Lord intends them to be in. While the teaching contained in this book may be new to some or even many, it truly reflects the Lord's desire and intention for His church. Only a person born of the Spirit of God can receive the things of God, and furthermore, only a person being led by the Spirit of God will allow them to be applied in his or her life.

Additionally the preaching of the gospel is the preaching of the cross. This was reflected in the life of John the Baptist when he openly declared, "He must increase, but I must decrease" (John 3:30). And Paul plainly tells the Corinthian church, "For Christ sent me … to preach the Gospel, not with wisdom of words, lest the cross of Christ should be made of none effect" (1 Corinthians 1:17). I know it is the earnest desire of the author that, as you read this book, you would find that pearl of great value that remains hidden until found by a seeking and hungry heart. In the light of the glory of God in the face of Jesus Christ, all things will grow dim and eventually disappear until we all come into the unity of the faith, thereby moving toward the Lord's true purpose for the church. Most assuredly, "the Spirit and the bride say come!" May we be found in agreement with the apostle John in response to this revelation of the Spirit when he said, "Even so, come Lord Jesus."

James Parnell
Teacher at Cornerstone Bible Center

\#\#\#

Alex Delpercio has been a personal friend of mine for many years. He has been a gifted Bible school teacher for more than twenty-eight years, and he is committed to the study of God's Word.

There are many years of experience and dedication to the Lord contained in this little book. I believe *Preparing the Bride of Christ* will be bread to hungry hearts, as well as an aid in Bible study and sermon preparation.

As you read this book, may God's Holy Spirit guide you into the truth written within. May it inspire you to give yourself wholly to the Lord as you endeavor to become part of the bride of Christ.

Pastor James Klein
Cornerstone Christian Fellowship

PREFACE

For some time I have been of the opinion that the last thing needed in Christianity today is another book. It seems as though everyone is writing books about everything, flooding the market with that which profits authors but has little or no eternal value. I have never intended to write a book on any subject, but a few years ago I taught a four-week class on the preparation of the bride of Christ and experienced a burden placed upon my heart by the Lord. Over time that burden continued to grow, and writing this book was birthed from "the burden of the word of the Lord" (Malachi 1:1 NKJV).

As the reader moves through the chapters, the content may seem unrelated to the subject, but remember that the Lord is in the process of preparing His bride and He uses many different methods to that end. Some of the things in this book will not be palatable to the carnal Christian, but these are necessary, especially today, because we need Christians without stunted growth, Christians who are not retarded in their spiritual maturity.

The ways of the Lord are much higher than ours and are not readily received by many Christians because His ways are so contrary to man's thinking and desires. But the spiritual man will learn and delight in the Word of the Lord after the inward man. Those who comprise the bride will move in His ways, even if they may not like the ways, and these ones will please the Lord and become what He has given His life to provide.

ACKNOWLEDGMENTS

I would like to acknowledge Charles Haun and Jacob Luffy, who faithfully taught the Word of God with unswerving dedication and through whom my life has been greatly enriched.

INTRODUCTION

For the Christian, preparing the bride of Christ is most important because of ignorance and many misunderstandings related to this subject. Many have received teaching that because they are saved, when they get to heaven, all the rewards and all that is prepared will be theirs and that they will be included in everything. One's thinking will determine what the heart will be set toward, whether it be the world, one's own pursuits, what one may think the Bible teaches, or the Lord.

The determining factor in preparing the bride of Christ is not by age, race, intelligence, or denomination. None of these means will play any part in how the Lord prepares a Christian. Rather the individual's heart condition will determine how Jesus Christ can change him or her.

This book will be more of a teaching tool than the normal book. It is not a how-to book, which seems to be popular with Christians. Instead it is meant to point to a relationship with Jesus Christ, who is the one who can teach the Christian what is needed through the uncovering of Himself (Galatians 1:12) so that we can move toward Him. This book could have easily become a three-hundred-page book, but the Lord has brought it forth simply and directly.

We will look at many scriptures to try to shed light on this important topic. We will address the following questions:

- Because a Christian has experienced salvation, does that mean that they are prepared?
- What does it mean to be prepared?
- Will all Christians be included in the marriage?
- What can I do? What should I do?

The answers to these questions, and what we believe in relation to them are of utmost importance regardless of one's denomination or affiliation. Our belief will determine to a great degree the direction we take in our Christian walk because we will act according to what we believe or do not believe. Some may have never heard of the preparation of the bride of Christ. Some may think they are already prepared, and others will look to the Lord to prepare their hearts and draw ever nearer to Him.

The self-centered, fleshly Christian will not want to hear the message in this book and will try to dismiss it. That is because the flesh does not want to die! Self-centeredness cannot remain when the Lord is at work in preparing the heart. This book is not for the faint of heart, but it can help to direct the hearts of the ones who desire the Lord and want to move on to a greater relationship with Him.

The Lord Jesus is at work today in the hearts and lives of those Christians who truly love Him (John 14:15). For those who are willing, the Lord is working to prepare them for the most important event of all. Nothing ever seen, heard, or experienced will be able to compare with the marriage of Jesus to His bride and the intimacy that will follow.

FOR WHOM IS THIS BOOK WRITTEN?

The writing of this book is for those who know the Lord Jesus Christ, those who have responded to the gospel and have a personal relationship with Him. Not all who say that they are Christians are true Christians, and not all who go to church really know Jesus. People who are considered good people may not know the Lord, and many religious people who may think that they will go to heaven may not. It is not enough to be a Christian, go to church, be a good person, or to be religious.

There was a man in the Bible—a religious leader whose name was Nicodemus. He came to Jesus by night and questioned Him about the miracles that he saw Jesus perform. Nicodemus reasoned that Jesus could not do these miracles unless God was with Him. But Jesus did not address Nicodemus's question about the miracles but instead said the unexpected. Jesus says that unless a man is born again, he cannot see or enter the kingdom of God (John 3:3, 5). This was a surprise to this Jewish ruler, who thought that he knew the way of salvation.

Many people today are in the same place as Nicodemus was and think that they know the way. Jesus is the way, the truth, and the life, and without Him, there is no other way that will take a person to the Father. What is the birth that Jesus was talking about with Nicodemus? It is not religion, for religion does not satisfy the longing of the soul. It is not works, for it is by grace that we are saved. It is not morality because morality cannot save. So what was Jesus saying?

In the physical, when birth occurs, a baby goes from one place of existence to a completely different place of existence. The baby is born into a place that is not even remotely similar. Spiritual birth is the same in that one goes from one place of existence to another. Through the preaching of the gospel, Jesus comes to man and waits for a response from his heart. When people respond to the Lord and receive Him as the sacrifice for their sins, the Holy Spirit performs the miracle of the new birth. You cannot explain this birth to someone who has never experienced it, but for the heart that is childlike, the new birth becomes a reality. Physical life begins by birth, and spiritual life also begins by birth.

Nicodemus, who was very religious, did not understand the new birth, and people cannot understand it today. This birth from above transcends understanding, for salvation is by His grace and we believe by faith. This birth is necessary. Why?

Because Jesus said that man must be born again. "Jesus answered and said to him, Most assuredly, I say to you, unless one is born again, he cannot see the kingdom of God" (John 3:3 NKJV). This birth is necessary because man cannot save himself. "For it is by grace you have been saved, through faith—and this not from yourselves, it is the gift of God—not by works, so that no one can boast" (Ephesians 2:8–9 NIV). It is necessary because man has a sinful nature. "For all have sinned, and come short of the glory of God" (Romans 3:23 KJV).

"But the scripture hath concluded all under sin" (Galatians 3:22 KJV). How can man be born again? He must acknowledge that he is a sinner and that he has a need for the Savior, repent of his sins, and sincerely receive Jesus Christ as his Savior.

> He came to His own, and His own did not receive Him. But as many as received Him, to them He gave the right to become children of God, to those who believe in His name: who were born, not of blood, nor of the will of the flesh, nor of the will of man, but of God. (John 1:11–13 NKJV)

If you have picked up this book and have never received Jesus as your Savior, I implore you to do so today, for today is the day of salvation. You will experience the new birth, and you will find true satisfaction. You will find purpose for your life, and then this book will apply to you! "For God so loved the world that He gave His only begotten Son, that whoever believes in Him should not perish but have everlasting life" (John 3:16 NKJV).

If you would like to receive Jesus Christ as your Savior, sincerely pray this prayer. "Lord Jesus, I believe you are the Son of God and died for me. I am a sinner, repent of my sins, and ask you to forgive me and come into my heart. By faith I receive you, Jesus, as my personal Lord and Savior."

"Whoever believes in the Son has eternal life, but whoever rejects the Son will not see life, for God's wrath remains on him" (John 3:36 NIV).

CHAPTER 1

THE GENERAL AND THE PERSONAL CALL OF GOD

The Lord Jesus Christ calls to all men in order to save them. Whoever wishes can come and drink of the water of life freely, for the Lord does not want man to perish. To all men God offers the great provision of salvation, but man's perspective keeps him from experiencing salvation. Some people see God as a hard and merciless God who does not care for creation or for the difficulties of man. But the Lord is merciful and caring, and He does not want man to go his own way. "The Lord is not slack concerning His promise, as some count slackness, but is longsuffering toward us, not willing that any should perish but that all should come to repentance" (2 Peter 3:9 NKJV).

As it is with a child who has left the family in poor standing, man may think that the Lord will not accept him again. The child may never know what is in the parent's heart unless he makes his way back home. God desires for man to come to Him and experience all that He has provided.

One of the essential points in the above verse is repentance, which is turning away from sin and turning back to God. Being truly sorry for sin and coming to Jesus Christ will change one's relationship with God. In this day and age many do not think that there is any need to repent. However, man cannot see the true heart of God without repentance. Provision for man's spiritual well-being is available by Jesus' death, and the invitation is open to everyone.

Consider the following passages: "For God so loved the world that He gave His only begotten Son, that whoever believes in Him should not perish but have everlasting life" (John 3:16 NKJV). "For there is no difference between Jew and Gentile—the same Lord is Lord of all and richly blesses all who call on Him, for everyone who calls on the name of the Lord will be saved" (Romans 10:12-13 NIV).

In the Old Testament there was a national call to Israel to be holy and to be a light to the Gentile nations. God called prophets, priests, and kings to be godly and to have a relationship with the Lord. Their example was to guide the nation of Israel into righteousness, and to be a standard to the Gentiles. The call to the sinner is different from the call to the Christian. Today the call to salvation through Jesus Christ is the first and general call of God to the sinner. To understand God's call on a personal level we must first answer the general call of God. To answer the call of God is to progress upward to a much higher place, to become something that the individual has never dreamed possible. Paul called it the "upward call" that is to be moved toward with intensity. He pursued his calling from Jesus and desired to fulfill it. "I press toward the goal for the prize of the upward call of God in Christ Jesus" (Philippians 3:14 NKJV).

But where do we as Christians start? The same place that the disciples did when Jesus passed by and called to them saying, "Follow me." They immediately left what they were doing and followed Him, not knowing where they were going or what that call even meant. The disciples continued to walk with Jesus and He brought them to a place in Him that they could never have imagined. As they walked with the Lord and moved in what they knew, His personal call began to unfold for them a little at a time.

Through the gospel, the Lord continues to call today, looking for hearts that will answer and begin a journey, and the respondent has no idea where that path will end. There are some necessary components that will help the Christian understand the personal call of God for his or her life. They are faith, obedience, and endurance.

Faith

Without faith it is impossible to please God. Yet one can have strong, unshakable faith in him or herself, others, riches, human ability, and many other things without having faith in God. Also, the Christian can have misguided faith in what God *does* instead of who He *is*. Some Christians even have faith in faith, that is, belief in one's own ability to have faith, instead of belief in the truth. This type of faith unknowingly misses seeing God as the true source and direction of faith. "But without faith it is impossible to please Him, for he who comes to God must believe that He is, and that He is a rewarder of those who diligently seek Him" (Hebrews 11:6 KJV). "Therefore, leaving the discussion of the elementary principles of Christ, let us go on to perfection, not laying again the foundation of repentance from dead works and of faith toward God" (Hebrews 6:1 NKJV).

There can be a subtle shift from seeking Him to seeking the gifts He gives, placing one's inner focus in the wrong direction. This is much more common than one would think because it does not appear as misguided. God does give gifts and does answer prayer, but nothing He does or gives should occupy the attention of our hearts. Rather they should direct us more toward Him. *He* should always be the focus of our hearts.

True faith will take us to places we do not know and even to places we do not want to go. Faith in God will open our eyes to the personal call of God. It will challenge us to operate in a place far above our individual abilities, and it will take faith in Him to remain and function there. Faith in anything other than God Himself will not be sufficient. "Most assuredly, I say to you, when you were younger, you girded yourself and walked where you wished; but when you are old, you will stretch out your hands, and another will gird you and carry you where you do not wish" (John 21:18 NKJV).

Abraham left Ur of the Chaldees not knowing where the Lord was taking him, but he believed God and the Lord considered Abraham's faith as righteous and took him to a higher spiritual place. Abraham's faith in God led him into circumstances that he would not have chosen and to places he would have never gone. Because of his faith in God, he went through the unbelievable to obtain the promise of God and became a blessing to the nations (Galatians 3:6–8).

The Lord led Joseph into and out of terrible circumstances (Genesis Ch. 37, 39–41). The Bible never states that Joseph complained or blamed God for his circumstances. He learned that the Lord was in control, and he maintained faith toward God through his difficulties and even attributed his troubles to the Lord. "And God sent me before you to preserve a posterity for you in the earth, and to save your lives by a great deliverance. So now it was not you who sent me here, but God; and He has made me a father to Pharaoh, and lord of all his house, and a ruler throughout all the land of Egypt" (Genesis 45:7–8 NKJV).

Joseph had faith in God to take him into and bring him out of whatever circumstance that was before him to continue to increase his faith and reveal the righteousness of God to him. As Joseph centered his faith upon God alone he saw the unfolding of the personal will of God for him (Genesis 41:52b).

Esther showed faith in God in a time when her life and the lives of the other Jews were being threatened. Faith took her to places she did not know. She never dreamed that she would go to King Ahasuerus' palace and become queen. Then faith took her where she did not want to go.

> Then Esther told them to reply to Mordecai: Go, gather all the Jews who are present in Shushan, and fast for me; neither eat nor drink for three days, night or day. My maids and I will fast likewise. And so I will go to the king, which is against the law; and if I perish, I perish! (Esther 4:15–16 NKJV)

Even though Esther's faith in God took her down a path that she did not want to go, God preserved her and the Jews of that time and revealed His personal will to her (Esther 4:14).

For Abraham, Joseph, Esther, and others in the Bible, faith became more than believing in God for something they wanted. Rather, through their faith in God, they saw Him as the source and the Lord was able to bring them to a deeper spiritual place.

Obedience

Without this single characteristic, which we see in the Lord, if lacking in the believer, one can miss God's personal call. Jesus calls us to the marriage, but in order to fulfill that call, we must respond to His personal call. As we fulfill that call we are changed into the image of Christ. We are not called to preaching, teaching, missionary work, saving souls, feeding the poor, or any other work the Lord leads us to do. Our call is not to the ministry as an end in itself. Our personal call—whatever it may be—is meant to work the character of Christ within and to ultimately prepare us for the greater purpose of marriage to Christ. Our personal obedience to Jesus will help prepare us and enable us to move toward what the Lord has intended.

We can trace the failure of the Israelites in the wilderness to their lack of obedience to the Lord, although the Lord called them to be a light to the Gentile nations and to possess the land, they never accomplished that call. The heart of the Father was to set them high above all nations of the earth, but their disobedience caused them to be defeated before their enemies.

We will not fare any better if disobedience is the mode in which we operate. We can read the Bible, see the mistakes of the Israelites, and unknowingly fall into the same pattern of doing the same thing that they did. Obedience is not just to be a word we use. It is to become a way of life! We are to learn obedience, and the method the Lord uses is not appealing to the flesh. "Though He were a Son, yet learned He obedience by the things which He suffered" (Hebrews 5:8 NKJV).

Carrying out the will and word of another is not easy for the self-centered individual. To obey the Lord and to deny one's own desires can be a source of personal suffering that not many are willing to endure. But being a willing servant will help to ensure that the learning process of obedience will be successful in fulfilling the personal will of God for us and ultimately in bringing us to the marriage.

Endurance

Being a Christian for years enables one to see certain detrimental characteristics that bring great loss. One of them is the lack of endurance that seems to affect so many that seemingly start so well. Without endurance, the Christian may walk with the Lord for a while and then slowly fade away, never again to be in the ranks of the faithful. It is very sad to see a believer, through an inconsistent walk with Christ, slowly drift away as a ship that has lost its mooring. This can be because "the testing of your faith develops perseverance" (James 1:3 NIV).

There are too many Christians who will not stay in the test, allowing it to bring the results desired by the Lord. The natural inclination is to do whatever one can do to get out of the trial and to bring some comfort to the carnal man, which unknowingly thwarts the arrangement of God to develop endurance. The testing of faith is to reveal if it is genuine and to develop endurance, which is necessary to remain in what the Lord personally calls you to.

Jesus continues to call to the Christian in hope that he or she hears and follows to discover His personal call to that person. "For many are called, but few are chosen" (Matthew 22:14 NKJV).

Many choose the road of sin only to fall short of the glory that the Lord wanted for them. The Lord calls, and many respond; however, few become the choice vessels that He has intended. This is not because the Lord is slack concerning His promises, but the many have other desires and interests that conflict with the Lord's personal call for them (Matthew 16:24). So the Lord turns to the few, which may not be His first choice, but because they were "good ground" and endured (Matthew 13:23), He is able to accomplish His high call and purpose in and through them. "But My servant Caleb, because he has a different spirit in him and has followed Me fully, I will bring into the land where he went, and his descendants shall inherit it" (Numbers 14:24 NKJV).

Endurance in the spirit of Caleb enabled him to wholly follow the Lord and go further than the many Israelites that the Lord called. Be assured that Caleb had his faith tested and he remained in the test until endurance had its perfect work in him.

Our walk with the Lord is to be consistent so that we are not vacillating back and forth between sin and obedience and between our own will and His. Many places in the Bible admonish the Christian to walk in a manner that is pleasing to the Lord. "I, therefore, the prisoner of the Lord, beseech you to walk worthy of the calling with which you were called" (Ephesians 4:1 NKJV).

In the life of a Christian there is to be a comparative value between his old life and where he is spiritually today, and a slow transformation in character should take place as he does those things that are worthy in the Lord's sight. "That you would walk worthy of God who calls you into His own kingdom and glory" (1 Thessalonians 2:12 NKJV).

Remember, the call of God is not to heaven! Heaven is included in the kingdom, but heaven is not to be a goal. We will be in heaven without placing our attention there. Jesus Christ is to be our goal. He is to be our desire, and He is to be our focus, not heaven! With the heart focused upon Jesus, we can respond to His call and begin to move toward the greater purpose of preparation for the marriage to Him.

CHAPTER 2

OUR RESPONSE

The call of God goes forth to "whosoever will" in hope that a good response would be forthcoming and the new creation would begin. Jesus gives a parable of the sower who sowed seed in the ground. The seed has the potential to bring forth something that is totally different in appearance than what is sown. So the seed is sown in the ground in hope that what is desired will be produced from that little seed. All the conditions must be correct to release the tremendous potential that is within the seed so that what grows is the increase of the Lord.

Jesus describes certain soil conditions—hard, stony, thorny, and good. They represent heart conditions that are present in men that will bring forth something of temporal or eternal value. In the natural, soil condition can change through work—tilling, breaking clods, adding nutrients, watering, etc., all to make the soil more receptive to the seed planted. If work does not progress, then the seed will never produce because the soil is not conducive to growth, no matter how many seeds the Lord plants.

When people genuinely come to Christ, many things occur within them, one of which is a desire for the Lord and His Word. Desire must be cultivated so that continued growth occurs and so that the heart remains soft and pliable. Although the Holy Spirit places desire in hearts, we must maintain that desire through a constant cooperation with the Lord. That is why in 1 Peter 2:2 "desire the pure milk of the Word," the Greek verb translated *desire* in English, is an imperative mood verb, which means we are commanded to desire the pure word of

God. The Lord does not command us to create desire for Him, but the command is for us to maintain the longing that He has placed within us by walking in the Spirit and not fulfilling the lust of our flesh.

The day that I gave my heart to Jesus immediately there was placed within me a hunger for Him and His Word. I knew little of God, Jesus, or the Holy Spirit, and I was so ignorant that I could not even look up a scripture in the Bible correctly and stumbled through it, trying to look up a verse. I had no understanding of anything spiritual, but I knew something had happened within me and began to trust the Lord to help and teach me. Later I realized that the Lord had placed this driving hunger in my heart that had to be nurture through His Word, church, fellowship, etc.

Not only is there to be a response to the gospel initially, but also there is to be a continual response to the Lord as He tries to bring the Christian to maturity. He will reveal His Word, personally uncover His will to us, and show the way in which we should walk. There will be things that we will not like, but there are central truths of the gospel that are key to our development.

For example, consider the following:

- denying ourselves and taking our cross (Mark 8:34)
- crucifying the flesh (Galatians 5:24; Romans 13:14)
- the surrender of our will (Luke 22:42)
- turning away from sin (Hebrews 10:26)
- considering yourselves dead to sin (Romans 6:11)
- putting the Lord before everyone (Luke 14:26)
- losing your life in this world (Matthew 16:25)
- being a partaker of His suffering (1 Peter 4:13)

As we look at this list, we can see that these are impossible for us to do. But if we respond to the Lord, He can do above whatever we thought possible, and as we live in the principles of the gospel, He can bring about the fulfillment intended. Our response to Jesus is important because without it there will never be the proper development He is after, and we will settle for something far less than what the Lord has for us.

There are many examples in the Bible of men and women who responded correctly to the Lord under very difficult circumstances and developed spiritually far beyond others who had the same opportunity. Consider the following figures:

- *Joshua and Caleb* were two shining examples of hearts that responded to the Lord in difficult times and became witnesses in their generation to what the Lord can do with hearts that respond to Him. They were the only two adults of their generation that entered the Promised Land.

- *Joseph* did nothing wrong but found himself in terrible circumstances and had to live in them in the prime of his life. Because of his response to the Lord, he came forth with a spirit that God used to sustain the known world.

- While he was a captive in Babylon, *Daniel* responded to the Lord. His response got him into—and out of—the lion's den. His three friends responded to the Lord and that took them into—and out of—the fiery furnace.

- *Esther* responded to the Lord when her life was on the line and saved the Jewish people from a plot to eliminate them.

- *Peter, James, John,* and the other apostles responded to the call of Jesus to "follow Me" and were changed forever and were instrumental in helping to change the lives of millions.

- *Saul* of Tarsus (whose name was changed to Paul after his encounter with Christ) was a Pharisee of Pharisees, zealous for the law and a persecutor of Christians. Paul's response to Jesus Christ not only changed his generation but also strongly influenced every generation. And through unswerving dedication and response to the Holy Spirit, he penned much of the New Testament.

Our Pursuits

One great hindrance to the correct response to the Lord is our own self-pursuits. There are many Christians who cannot tell the difference between their pursuits and the Lord's will for them. Have you ever wondered what the will of God is for your life? The Bible gives direction that will help place the heart in a position that will make it easier for the Lord to reveal His will. "For this is the will of God, your sanctification" (1 Thessalonians 4:3 NKJV). "For this is the will of God, that you should be consecrated (separated and set apart for pure and holy living): that you should abstain and shrink from all sexual vice" (1 Thessalonians 4:3 AMP).

The importance for the Christian to separate from the world cannot be overstated. That does not mean that we should not be among unsaved people. Rather in our hearts we are to separate from worldly thinking and attitudes that will result in compromise and spiritual death. "Therefore Come out from among them and be separate, says the Lord. Do not touch what is unclean, and I will receive you. I will be a Father to you, and you shall be My sons and daughters, says the Lord Almighty" (2 Corinthians 6:17–18 NKJV).

To come out from among them, as this scripture says, does not mean we are not to be around people. We are in the world, but we are not to be of the world. The Christian is to be detached from anything that can stand between his heart and the Lord. Separation is internal, where no one sees but God. The evidence of separation is seen by walking with the Lord in a way not understood by the world.

When the Lord says, "I will receive you," this is not referring to initial salvation. It is talking about those who have become sons and daughters (not children), those who have come to maturity through the process of their separation and have intimate relationships with the Lord and relate to Him as Father.

In Romans 12:1–2, Paul gives three important statements to the church at Rome.

1) "Present your bodies a living sacrifice" (The word *living* is a participle, which means we are to do this continually.)
2) "Do not be conformed to this world" (The word *conformed* is in the imperative mood, which is a command.)
3) "Be transformed by the renewing of your mind" (The phrase "be transformed" is also a command.)

If we do not follow these three things, we will never be able to discern what the will of God is for us and will flounder around and live under our own thinking, presuming we are in the will of God. If the Christian does these things, he will be able to prove (determine) the will of God for his life. "And do not be conformed to this world, but be transformed by the renewing of your mind, that you may prove what is that good and acceptable and perfect will of God" (Romans 12:2 NKJV).

The heart can pursue God or pursue some earthly desire that may not appear to be evil but can take our attention off the Lord. The focus of the Christian's heart is to be Jesus, and if that is correct, then the heart can move toward Him without ceasing. What occupies our thinking, and what do we give ourselves to? What we give our time and attention to will reveal to us what we think is important and what our focus really is. Many Christians do not like to think that certain scriptures may relate to them, especially if the verses suggest corrections or do not contain what they consider to be blessing. "Because you say, 'I am rich, have become wealthy, and have need of nothing'—and do not know that you are wretched, miserable, poor, blind, and naked" (Revelation 3:17 NKJV).

Jesus said, "Because you say, I am rich." Apparently the Laodicean church had acquired wealth and may have thought that they were doing well or had been taught that to financially prosper is the blessing of the Lord. But in Jesus' estimation they were poor. They may have been quite surprised to receive these words of discipline and may have tried to trace back to where they began to err. True blessing is to prosper inwardly. "I counsel you to buy from Me gold refined in the fire, that you may be rich; and white garments, that you may be clothed, that the shame of your nakedness may not be revealed; and anoint your eyes with eye salve, that you may see" (Revelation 3:18 NKJV).

What is the gold that Jesus spoke of, and how can the Christian purchase it? The purchase of gold will be with your life, will, surrender, and time. We have the power to give these commodities to the Lord even though we may think the price is too dear. Jesus will exchange them for that which has great spiritual value. The gold refers to our faith and the value produced in the heart of those who cooperate with the Lord.

> In this you greatly rejoice, though now for a little while,
> if need be, you have been grieved by various trials, that
> the genuineness of your faith, being much more precious
> than gold that perishes, though it is tested by fire, may
> be found to praise, honor, and glory at the revelation of
> Jesus Christ. (1 Peter 1:6–7 NKJV)

The faith that the Lord is looking for is the faith that can stand in any trial. To take us from faith to *faith* will mean that it will be necessary to experience trials that push us to the very limit. As the Christian undergoes the testing of his faith (James 1:3), endurance is developed, and the faith that remains will be more precious than gold in God's sight. And the refining in the fire will produce quality within that was not there before. In the above verse, the phrase "may be found" testifies to the work that trials and fire can do in the heart.

When the heart is tied to self-pursuits, the work of the Lord within is frustrated, and what should have been accomplished remains unfinished.

The Bible gives examples of those who had self-pursuits that became sources of destruction to them in their lives.

1) Even though God used Samson greatly, his interest was in what pleased him and not what pleased the Lord. Samson's pursuits

became his undoing, and they brought great destruction to the life of a man who could have risen to greatness.

Judges 14:1–3
>   (v1) "Samson… saw …"
>   (v2) "I have seen…get her (Delilah) for me …"
>   (v3) "get her (Delilah) for me for she pleases me well"

Samson was interested in self-pursuits instead of asking God for direction. His obstinate determination would eventually lead to his downfall.

Judges 16:1, 4
>   (v1) "Samson… saw a harlot there, and went in to her."
>   (v4) "Afterward it happened that he loved a woman in the Valley of Sorek, whose name was Delilah."

Choosing a harlot to lie with and then choosing Delilah reveals that Samson pursued what he wanted and not what pleases the Lord.

2) By reading some of the things the prophet Balaam said, it seems as though his pursuits were correct (Numbers 22:18). But he shows Balak how to make Israel stumble, and his pursuit of reward caused him to forsake the right way and respond incorrectly to the Lord (2 Peter 2:15; Jude 11).

3) Jesus reprimanded the Pharisees for their pursuits of the most honorable seats in the synagogues rather than seeking after God (Luke 11:43). Their desires led them to seek reputation and attention. This same thing has become popular in the church today and is lauded by many as being spiritual, but if self-interest is moving in the heart, it becomes a destructive pursuit.

4) It appeared that Judas Iscariot was sincere in his walk with Jesus (John 12:5–6), but what was in his heart was revealed later. His

pursuit of money drove him down a different path that led him to ruin (Matthew 27:5).

5) The rich young ruler, who Jesus possibly considered for the position vacated by Judas, did not respond to Jesus' invitation to follow Him because he had great riches. He had other interests (Matthew 19:22).

In the above examples, there was lack of response to the Lord that resulted in spiritual loss for the individual. At the time it did not appear to be loss. Rather it appears to be gain. Their self-pursuits caused them to lose out for all eternity because the work that the Lord wanted to do in their hearts remained unaccomplished. "There is a way that seems right to a man, But its end is the way of death" (Proverbs 14:12 NKJV). "They would none of my counsel: they despised all my reproof. Therefore shall they eat of the fruit of their own way, and be filled with their own devices" (Proverbs 1:30–31 KJV).

You can also consider this passage: "Do not be deceived, God is not mocked; for whatever a man sows, that he will also reap. For he who sows to his flesh will of the flesh reap corruption, but he who sows to the Spirit will of the Spirit reap everlasting life" (Galatians 6:7–8 NKJV).

Sowing to the Spirit will guarantee the Christian quality of life and the everlasting life that God promises.

Come

"And the Spirit and the bride say, Come. And let him who hears say Come. And let him who thirsts come" (Revelation 22:17 NKJV).

The Spirit and the completed bride say come. The call moves back in time from the union to warn and encourage a response. *Come* is the call coming out from the hearts of those who have answered the call, and became the bride of Christ, and experienced relationship with the Lord that is so good that there is a cry to others to come and experience the same. In this verse there is complete unity between the Spirit and the bride. This results in the union that is far above what man has ever thought possible. It is so good, pure, right, and wonderful that the strongest possible language is used. It is a command repeated three times. *Come! Come! Come!* "And let him who hears say, "Come!" And let him who thirsts come" (Revelation 22:17 NKJV). Hearing is necessary to direct one's life in this direction. Those who hear and respond the Lord can bring toward the union. *Thirsts* (a participle) is to be continual, so that Jesus draws the heart and He becomes the center of one's life.

Not all Christians are the same. Not all respond or want to respond to the Lord, and so too is the level to which they can be brought along. We are to see the marriage in spirit and move toward it in faith!

Response to the Lord is huge and not given enough consideration by Christians. Will there be good or bad soil? Will there be openness between your heart and the Holy Spirit? Will the Lord be able to work through your circumstances? Can we receive from the hand of the Lord what He desires instead of what we want? Will we prepare for the marriage? We will find the answers to these questions through our response or lack of response to the Lord.

As the Spirit and the bride say, "Come," it will take a special heart to answer that call. People in every age have had the opportunity to hear and to cooperate with the Lord in the process that can make them ready. We must set our hearts toward Jesus Christ, surrender and respond to Him, and allow the Holy Spirit to work in us to make the necessary changes and prepare us for the marriage to Jesus Christ!

CHAPTER 3

PROGRESSION

Some things in the Bible are not well defined, and the Lord hides some truths so that seeing them will take a work of the Holy Spirit within along with revelation from the Lord. One can glimpse a certain truth and yet see it fade as one tries to follow it in the scriptures because it moves deeper than the individual's revelation. That does not mean that it is not true. Rather it testifies that revelation is progressive and can await the heart that presses on to know the Lord. Usually if a truth is not well defined, it is placed aside and considered a fringe element and kept out because it is not in one's realm of understanding or experience. But certain truth plays an important role in determining the direction that the heart goes and helps to point the Christian toward a greater relationship with Jesus, even though it is not as concrete as some think it should be.

There is a mind-set in Christianity that being saved is all that is necessary and that when Christians get to heaven, they will be included in everything that goes on. All the rewards will be theirs, and there will be nothing further needed after they accept Christ. If that were true, then why even be concerned with desiring a closer walk with Jesus, doing good works, being separate from the world, denying self, and the leading of the Spirit? What is the point in living under restriction and not fulfilling one's own desires if Christians receive everything because of initial salvation? This thinking is the norm in different churches and causes many to live in a lackadaisical way instead of walking diligently (Ephesians 5:15).

There are words in the Bible that Christians treat as synonyms even though different Greek words are used. Sometimes this can be correct, and different words can be used interchangeably and relate to each other; however, this is not always the case. There can be an important distinction, which can portray some hidden truth.

There is an important question to consider. Is being saved and being birthed into the kingdom the same thing, or is there a difference between the two? And if there is a difference, is it significant enough to even pay attention to?

Consider this: In the Bible there is only one qualification to be saved, but there are many qualifications related to the kingdom. The only qualification on being saved is calling upon the name of the Lord. In the New Testament no other qualifications are mentioned. "For whosoever shall call upon the name of the Lord shall be saved" (Romans 10:13 KJV). (See also Acts 2:21; Joel 2:32; and Acts 4:12.)

But when Jesus talks with Nicodemus, He was specifically talking about the kingdom. Jesus was trying to show Nicodemus where someone who was a ruler and teacher of the Jews in spirit should be functioning (John 3:10). "Unless one is born again, he cannot see the kingdom of God" (John 3:3 NKJV).

A birth must take place in order to see or perceive the kingdom of God. "Unless one is born of water and the Spirit, he cannot enter the kingdom of God" (John 3:5 NKJV).

A birth must take place in order to enter the kingdom of God. The word *enter* in Greek is pronounced in English ice-er-khom-ahee, and it is the formation of two Greek words, the preposition *eis*, meaning *into*, and *erchomai*, meaning "to come from one place into another, to come into."

Unlike being saved, when the kingdom of God is mentioned in the scriptures, there are many different qualifications. For example, there must be *dedication* to the kingdom. "And Jesus said unto him, No man, having put his hand to the plough, and looking back, is fit for the kingdom of God" (Luke 9:62 KJV).

> So He said to them, Assuredly, I say to you, there is no one who has left house or parents or brothers or wife or children, for the sake of the kingdom of God, who shall not receive many times more in this present time, and in the age to come eternal life. (Luke 18:29–30 NKJV)

Without dedication, one will not set his heart toward the kingdom and will not even be interested in the kingdom.

There is *cost* involved. "Again, the kingdom of heaven is like treasure hidden in a field, which a man found and hid; and for joy over it he goes and sells all that he has and buys that field" (Matthew 13:44 NKJV). There is no personal cost to call upon the name of the Lord to be saved, but the kingdom may cost all that one has.

Those who are reduced (poor) possess the kingdom. "Blessed are the poor in spirit, for theirs is the kingdom of heaven" (Matthew 5:3 NKJV). The poor in spirit depend on the Lord, and that dependency is what makes the kingdom available to them.

It will take *tribulation* or pressure to enter the kingdom. "We must through much tribulation enter into the kingdom of God" (Acts 14:22 KJV). The Bible does not teach that we are saved through much tribulation, but tribulation accompanies entrance to the kingdom.

The kingdom will require some type of *suffering*. "Which is manifest evidence of the righteous judgment of God, that you may be counted worthy of the kingdom of God, for which you also suffer" (2 Thessalonians 1:5 NKJV). Persecution and tribulation cannot be divorced from the gospel, and suffering cannot be separate from the kingdom.

The kingdom will demand the *preeminence* in one's life. "But seek first the kingdom of God and His righteousness, and all these things shall be added to you" (Matthew 6:33 NKJV). Without the kingdom being first in the heart and thinking, there cannot be the increase the Lord desires for the Christian.

The above scriptures are not talking about being saved but are laying forth that which is necessary to progress in the kingdom of God. It seems as though there may be some difference between calling on the name of the Lord to be saved and moving in the kingdom. One can be saved and not move under kingdom principles. That does not mean that the person is unsaved, but possibly they have not moved into this other area. They have not entered the kingdom and do not function there (John 3:5).

Have you ever talked about spiritual things with someone who was saved and who relates everything you say to the natural or to his or her own understanding and reasoning? This person knows nothing about walking in the Spirit, the leading of the Lord, and the communication of the Spirit, and it is as if you are speaking a very different language to the individual. It is possible that he or she did not experience birth into the kingdom realm, where they would perceive these things. Are they saved?

Some would say no, but that may not be the case. I have seen individuals who genuinely called upon the name of the Lord and were saved, and this was evidenced by them saying things no unsaved person would say; however, they never progressed into the kingdom realm. Some call on the name of the Lord but never move toward the kingdom. Being saved and being birthed into the kingdom should take place simultaneously, and most of the time they do; however, that may not be the case with some.

There are also factors that will disqualify or hinder one from moving into the kingdom. The attitude of the Pharisees disqualified them from the kingdom (John 8:41). The religious leaders had a negative mindset toward the gospel Jesus proclaimed, and would not receive the teaching about the kingdom. John the Baptist came in the way of righteousness, Jesus came in the way of righteousness, and still the Pharisees did not believe them. Their unrighteousness made them unfit for the kingdom of God.

Paul wrote to the Corinthian church and exposed their behavior by saying that they did wrong by cheating their brothers (1 Corinthians 6:8). He knew that immoral conduct not corrected would disrupt their growth in the kingdom. Paul tries to correct their conduct by comparing their behavior to the unrighteous, who will not inherit the kingdom of God.

> Do you not know that the unrighteous will not inherit the kingdom of God? Do not be deceived. Neither fornicators, nor idolaters, nor adulterers, nor homosexuals, nor sodomites, nor thieves, nor covetous, nor drunkards, nor revilers, nor extortioners will inherit the kingdom of God. (1 Corinthians 6:9–10 NKJV)

Another disqualifying factor is the reliance on riches. The Bible does not teach that money is wrong; rather, it is the love of money that is the root of all evil. "How hard is it for them that trust in riches to enter into the kingdom of God" (Mark 10:24 KJV). Anyone who trusts in riches instead of the Lord will be hindered from entering (like the rich young ruler in Matthew 19:23).

Not all Christians are the same. Not all Christians cooperate in the arrangements of God. Some become drunk on their own will and what they desire to do with their lives. Disciples are not necessarily the same as believers. Disciples are believers, but not all believers are necessarily disciples. "Then said Jesus to those Jews which believed on Him, If ye continue in My Word, then are ye My disciples indeed" (John 8:31 KJV). One can believe in Jesus and not be a disciple of Jesus. Jesus said to these Jews who believed, that to become His disciples they must abide in His Word. Without continuing or abiding, they would not move toward discipleship, but instead remain believers.

Jesus teaches the same thing elsewhere in the New Testament. "If anyone comes to Me and does not hate his father and mother, wife and children, brothers and sisters, yes, and his own life also, he cannot be My disciple. And whoever does not bear his cross and come after Me cannot be My disciple" (Luke 14:26–27 NKJV).

If anyone wants to be a disciple of Jesus and loves father, mother, wife, children or anyone more than Him, including his own life, he cannot be Jesus' disciple. No one who places a higher value on earthly relationships than on being a disciple can be a disciple of Christ. This teaches that there is more involved in the Christian walk than just being saved.

Another scripture that points to these two areas is John 10:9. We must understand that when the Bible is (and was) translated into English, the translators strive to bring forth a Bible that is readable to the masses. So they use common grammar rules that they apply to the translation. For example, if you were to write a paragraph, the rules of composition would dictate that you would not use the same word repeatedly. The use of synonyms is to prevent repetition of the same word so that the paragraph is more readable. This is the approach used in translation so that there is a better flow. But examining the Greek text and seeing the same word used multiple times draws attention to some truth that may not be seen in English. "I am the door: by me if any man enter in, he shall be saved, and shall go in and out, and find pasture" (John 10:9 KJV).

In the English translation of John 10:9, unless one goes to the Greek they will miss an important truth. In this verse there are two entrances. The Greek word #1525 appears two times in this verse (Strong's, 1995).

(John 10:9 KJV)

1) "enter in …" (1525)— This entrance is for salvation. "if any man enter in, he shall be saved."
2) "shall go in" (1525)—This is a middle-voice verb, which indicates the subject performing an action upon himself or for his own benefit. (There is no middle voice in English). The subject (the saved one) enters into this place of pasture (feeding, growth, or increase) for his or her own benefit.

There are clearly two entrances in this verse. The first is for salvation and the second entrance seems to be something further on, a progression into something more than initial salvation. Some Christians are satisfied to remain in a place of lesser fulfillment in order to avoid the personal responsibilities of moving forward, growing, and seeking the Lord. "I am come that they might have life." (This is the first entrance.) "And that they might have it more abundantly." (This is the second entrance.) (See John 10:10 KJV.)

Having life from God is exciting, but pressing forward to acquire abundant life may not be as exciting because there will be personal cost involved, which many are not willing to pay. The Christian that thinks, *I am saved. I am going to heaven, and that is all there is to being a Christian,* may be robbing him or herself of great spiritual riches that the Lord wants to place within the person. Being saved will take us to heaven, but entering the kingdom of God will take us deeper in Christ!

God has created growth, and He places it in a little baby. And the result is seen in the child's physical development. It will be normal for the infant to grow and mature if you give the baby food, water, shelter, clothing, and love. But in the spiritual realm there are some differences. There is a phenomenon in Christianity today that is not recognized as a problem. Many Christians have stunted growth and retarded maturity, and no one seems to be alarmed! Christians can go from being young to old in a state of underdevelopment, and the sad thing is that they can be completely unaware of it.

There are some key elements found in the Bible related to growth that will result in a lack of or no growth at all if missing. One of those elements is desire. We are to have great affection and longing for the Word of God and settle for no other substitutes. "As newborn babes, desire the pure milk of the word, that you may grow thereby" (1 Peter 2:2 NKJV).

Newborn babies have intense desires for milk because their bodies know that they cannot survive without it. Physical hunger is one of the most compelling desires that a person can experience. We have heard stories of what people did because of the driving force of hunger, things that were unthinkable. God tells Israel that if they are disobedient, their enemies will defeat them, and they will do the unthinkable and eat their children in the siege (Deuteronomy 28:54–57). This actually took place when Ben-hadad besieged Samaria (2 Kings 6:28–29).

So too we are to have an intense desire for God's Word. One difference is that some Christians do not know that the new creature cannot live without the Word. We can compare feeding upon God's Word to feeding in order to maintain our bodies, but there is a much greater need for spiritual feeding. Job saw the greater importance of the spiritual man when he said, "I have esteemed the words of his mouth more than my necessary food" (Job 23:12 KJV). This is quite a testimony that Job treasured the Word of the Lord more than the food that his body needed. Spiritual hunger can be quite compelling. In the wilderness when Satan tempted Jesus, the Lord valued the Word of God more than physical bread.

When we were born again, God placed a hunger for the Word within our hearts. The incorruptible seed placed within you will not decay or die. It is not subject to the decay and the death that we see in this world. This hunger is satisfied through feeding upon the bread that the Lord gives. "Give us this day our daily bread" (Matthew 6:11 KJV).

This daily bread is what Christians need to enable them to develop properly. The necessary food that Job talks about (Job 23:12) is the prescribed portion that God chooses to give when He chooses. This feeding will result in growth. Growth leads to maturity and progression in the kingdom of God. Without hunger, the Christian will not progress in his or her relationship to the Lord and will not progress in the kingdom of God. But those who hunger for the Lord will progress in their spiritual development, and that relationship with the Lord will be what brings them into the marriage. "Blessed are you who hunger now, for you shall be filled" (Luke 6:21 NKJV).

CHAPTER 4

BECOMING

Have you ever heard someone say, "I do not know the purpose of God for my life?" When Christians say they do not know God's purpose for their life, usually they relate that to doing something for God. We are first called to become and then to do! Most know Matthew 4:19, which says, "Follow me, and I will make you fishers of men," and often Christians quote this verse. But in Mark 1:17, the same verse is written with the addition of one Greek word. This word is very significant and adds to this scripture a different dimension oftentimes missed. "Follow Me, and I will make you become fishers of men" (Mark 1:17 NKJV).

The word is *become*! Most of the time these verses are used when one is dealing with the thought of winning souls as fishermen catch fish. Many times new converts want to go out and win souls for Christ before much has developed in them. For the Christian *to become* is very important because the character of the witness can determine the quality of the convert. "Yields seed according to its kind" (Genesis 1:12 NKJV). There is a shallowness in Christians today that is accepted as the norm because it is not seen as shallowness. There is lack of desire to know the Lord, to press on toward Him, and to know Him in a more intimate way. Christians are satisfied with just making it to heaven and have little concern for maturing and having spiritual substance to use to minister to others. Some believers do not even realize that there is more that the Lord has for them beyond initial salvation.

The simplest meaning of the word *become* is "to be made," and making is a process. At initial salvation, the Lord brought us from lives of sin and birthed us into Him with the intent that we would go from being babes to spiritually grown men and women. It is the desire of God for the Christian to develop correctly and become of finer quality. But how can this take place?

Surrender

Adam and Eve had the choice to surrender to God and obey what He said to them. We know that they did not surrender, and sin and death passed upon all men as a result. We have the same choice available today. We also decide whether we will obey God or not.

The Christian faces many choices. Some are not too crucial, and other choices are very important. What people yield to will either prepare them for intimacy with the Lord or keep them from a close relationship. "Neither yield ye your members as instruments of unrighteousness unto sin: but yield yourselves unto God" (Romans 6:13 KJV).

When Jesus came by and called to Simon and Andrew to become fishers of men, they answered this call by leaving their nets and following (e.g., surrendering to the Lord). This was just the first of many ways the Lord would require them to yield to Him. Surrender starts small and slow, and then it becomes like a snowball rolling down a hill, gaining momentum and substance and eventually turning into an avalanche. Jesus requires all—total surrender from His disciples.

Surrender is not natural, and many times men are not too fond of being in a place of submission. As Christians, we also may not want to surrender our lives fully to the Lord for fear of the unknown or surrender to those who are over us. But surrender runs deep into the heart to the place that most do not want the Lord to intrude, where we say, "Lord, anything but that! I will surrender in some other area, but I do not want to surrender to what You are asking today." "Submit yourselves therefore to God" (James 4:7 KJV).

In this verse the word *submit* is a command to become passive to the Lord's desires and will. Even though we may know this, we can still have trouble following this directive and giving control to the Lord. Surrender allows the Spirit to lead us and to bring us into the arrangements of God for our lives.

In this day and age submission has become a word that is looked upon with disdain. Because of its many abuses by those who do not understand how submission is to operate, many do not see the value or purpose in submitting to God, a husband, a boss, or authorities. Lack of surrender has brought great spiritual destruction upon those who will not come under its power. The teaching of the New Testament and the example of Jesus show that self-surrender is necessary for the disciple. "And he who does not take his cross and follow after Me is not worthy of Me" (Matthew 10:38 NKJV). "And whoever does not bear his cross and come after Me cannot be My disciple" (Luke 14:27 NKJV).

The Lord desires to see the Christian become what He has planned, but we can fight against God if we are not willing to submit to His leading and if we persist in our own ways. This process of becoming is slow and arduous and will require the Christian submission that continues to grow deeper and wider and become fuller. The value that can be found through yielding to the Lord may never be realized with some, and their personal development may never be realized because of unwilling hearts. We cannot be Jesus' disciples unless we have hearts that are willing to submit. We may be Christians who will make it to heaven, but as far as becoming what He wants and maturing in our walk, we will fall short.

Being Conformed

There is something going on in the world that is not apparent to most people because of the blindness of man.

> But if our gospel be hid, it is hid to them that are lost:
> In whom the god of this world hath blinded the minds
> of them which believe not, lest the light of the glorious

gospel of Christ, who is the image of God, should shine
unto them. (2 Corinthians 4:3-4 KJV)

Everyone is being conformed to something! To be conformed is
to become similar in form, nature, or character. Man was born with
a sinful nature (fallen nature) that is the same as the nature of Adam,
and because of that, he cannot help but sin. The sinful nature will keep
man in bondage to his nature and keep the character of Adam alive.
The world is being conformed to the image of the god of this world—
Satan. Whether people believe that or not, that does not change the
truth. Satan was a liar from the beginning. He steals, kills, and destroys
whatever and whoever he can. We can see that same nature to varying
degrees in those who are being conformed to Satan's image. What
people give their attention to will determine what they become. Those of
the world beholding others who carry the character of the fallen nature
and desiring to become like them will to some degree become like that
which they see.

As Christians, we should not to allow the world to shape and
mold us after the pattern of the world but to become something quite
different. "And do not be conformed to this world, but be transformed
by the renewing of your mind, that you may prove what is that good
and acceptable and perfect will of God" (Romans 12:2 NKJV).

Renewing the mind can only occur through surrendering to the
Word of God, allowing within a transformation to take place. What
one beholds is important because he or she will change into that which
the person beholds. The Christian is to behold Jesus, which will be the
first step in becoming like Him. But what does it mean to behold, and
how do we do that? "But we all, with unveiled face, beholding as in a
mirror the glory of the Lord, are being transformed into the same image
from glory to glory, just as by the Spirit of the Lord" (2 Corinthians
3:18 NKJV).

To understand the intent of beholding the Lord, we must examine
the Greek verb and its inflections. The English word *beholding* used to
translate the Greek verb is a present participle, middle-voice verb. The

present participle, which is shown by using the suffix -ing, shows that the Christian is to presently and continually behold (or place his or her eyes upon) the Lord Jesus Christ. Middle voice means that the subject (the one beholding Jesus) does this for his or her own benefit.

Beholding is a continual inner direction of the heart, a poise of the spirit that holds Christ as the center so that it becomes possible to see His glory. As the inner man looks at Jesus, the Christian is gradually transformed (a form of the word *metamorphosis*) into the image of Jesus, the one whom he or she is beholding.

There is another important thing to see in this scripture. The word *unveiled* speaks of the heart of the individual who sees his or her true self as the Lord reveals that to the person. This draws a sharp contrast between the human heart and the heart of the Lord so that the Christian sees how far short he or she falls and how far above the individual Jesus really is.

Peter, James, and John were not aware of what glory was contained within Jesus, but when they saw Him transfigured before them, they were so astonished that Peter, not knowing what to say, suggested making three tabernacles. The veil of flesh (His body) changed before them so that the glory of God emanated from within Jesus. "Beloved, now are we the sons of God, and it doth not yet appear what we shall be: but we know that, when he shall appear, we shall be like him" (1 John 3:2 KJV).

We do not know the extent to which inner change will occur in us, but we do have opportunities today to allow the Lord to work in our hearts to bring about the metamorphosis that He desires. Do all circumstances work for the Christian's good? Do all things work for good for *all* Christians? Our initial thought may be yes, but what does the Bible say? "And we know that all things work together for good to those who love God, to those who are the called according to His purpose. For whom He foreknew, He also predestined to be conformed to the image of His Son" (Romans 8:28–29 NKJV).

It is important to read the scripture and not assume that we know what it says. Verse 28 says, "all things work together for good to those who love God." The next question we should ask is this: Do all Christians love God? Jesus clearly said, "If anyone loves Me, he will keep My word" (John 14:23 NKJV). All things do not work together for good for all Christians, but for those who love God and keep His commandments, they will be the ones who are interested in the Lord, His purpose for them, and becoming like Him (Romans 8:29). Being conformed to the image of Jesus is upon the heart of the Father, and He will work to accomplish this in the lives of those Christians who love Him.

Suffering

No one likes to suffer, and we do not even like the thought of suffering in any way. But man will inevitably experience suffering of some kind. Everyone born into this world will experience suffering. "But man is born to trouble as the sparks and the flames fly upward" (Job 5:7 AMP).

The Christian has a distinct advantage because he can suffer according to the will of God. Suffering does not necessarily produce godly qualities because there are varying reasons why one can be suffering:

1) Those who do not know Christ in a personal way suffer in vain because their suffering produces nothing of eternal value in them. They go through some of the same things Christians do, but their suffering does not develop the character of Jesus Christ within, so their suffering may only help them in this life.

2) Sometimes Christians cause their own suffering because of the decisions they make. They either exclude the Lord from their decisions, knowingly or unknowingly, or they just decide their own direction and bring suffering and difficulty upon themselves. They will reap very little of eternal value from their suffering.

3) Then there are those Christians who suffer according to the will of God. They walk with God, allow the Holy Spirit to lead them and experience suffering in this way, and reap much fruit. These ones will receive much from the Lord and will take with them that which is of great eternal value.

The sufferings of this present time are to produce the glory of God within us. Jesus brings us into circumstances that have the potential to bring great spiritual wealth. He wants to make us become like Him so that when we leave this life, we take with us something of value. That is why we are to continually behold Him so that we can be transformed into His image and glean from our circumstances and receive from Him what we could not receive any other way. "For unto you it is given in the behalf of Christ, not only to believe on Him, but also to suffer for His sake" (Philippians 1:29 KJV).

Christians do not need to look for suffering. We just need to walk with God, for suffering will find us. The Bible gives many examples of men and women who suffered for the Lord, and church history has many who suffered and died as a result of living and walking with God. "Wherefore let them that suffer according to the will of God commit the keeping of their souls to Him in well doing, as unto a faithful Creator" (1 Peter 4:19 KJV).

The Apostle Paul lists some of his sufferings in the will of God (2 Corinthians 11:23–28). He was in prison, flogged, and exposed to death repeatedly. Five times he received thirty-nine lashes, three times beaten with rods, once stoned, and three times shipwrecked. He spent a day and a night in the open sea. He has been in danger from rivers, bandits, his own countrymen, and the Gentiles. Paul was in danger in the city, in danger in the country, in danger at sea, and in danger from false brothers. He had gone without sleep, known hunger and thirst, gone without food, was cold and naked, and experienced the daily pressure of his concerns for all the churches.

Looking at the things Paul had to suffer and looking at our lives, we will see that some of the things we face are not so bad. It is no wonder that Paul had so much in God to offer others. He puts all his sufferings in perspective! "For I reckon that the sufferings of this present time are not worthy to be compared with the glory which shall be revealed in us" (Romans 8:18 KJV).

This is a very revealing scripture if we see what Paul is saying. Firstly all the suffering in the will of God brought upon us through the leading and work of the Spirit will be one of the means the Lord uses to take His glory and place it within the Christian. Most will try to avoid suffering because it is normal to do so. However, the Lord has ways that make avoidance impossible. Secondly Paul considered that if he were to place all his sufferings on one side of a scale and the glory of the Lord placed in him on the other side, there would be no comparison.

Today we see a great lack of teaching regarding suffering, testing, tribulation, death to self, and other important aspects of the gospel, which can hurt the body of Christ. Many do not consider these teachings positive and encouraging, but that view comes forth from carnal thinking. Suffering should not be divorced from the gospel and be treated as a negative element that should be left out because some preachers feel it is not an encouraging subject. This thinking leads to preaching another gospel, which robs Christians of the opportunity to cooperate with the Lord and to develop spiritually as the Lord intends. Suffering can silence the self inside of us, which is very beneficial.

Testing

One of the processes the Lord uses to develop Christian character is testing. In the Bible we see the words *trial, try, trying, test,* and *testing* used in the Old and New Testament, each referring to the Lord testing the individual. The growth of Christian character is important and necessary if there is to be hearts within us that resemble the Lord Jesus. Not all Christians direct their hearts toward the Lord. Not all have a strong desire to know Him in a closer relationship, and not all will pay the price for that spiritual value. "The refining pot is for silver and the furnace for gold, but the Lord tests the hearts" (Proverbs 17:3 NKJV).

Even though we do not like tests and will do what we can to avoid them, Jesus is faithful to bring what He deems necessary so that we have the opportunity to see what really is in our hearts. Testing will reveal what is truly within us (Deuteronomy 8:2) and can give direction as to the remedy we need so that further growth can continue. Being in a test does not mean that the Christian is not in the will of God. Rather it is in the will of God that we should encounter tests because these have the potential to produce His character within us (Romans 5:3–4 NKJV). "Knowing that the testing of your faith produces patience" (James 1:3 NKJV). "Beloved, think it not strange concerning the fiery trial which is to try you, as though some strange thing happened unto you" (1 Peter 4:12 KJV).

Some think that the trials of life do not produce anything of value and are only sources of aggravation and agitation that we should avoid because life has enough problems. The carnal Christian will never see the value of tests. This person will not submit to God because he or she is of worldly thinking and wants to save his or her life in this world. But Jesus said that those who save their lives in this world will lose it.

The fire in the trial is like a smith who puts gold or silver in the fire to burn out the impurities. The fire is to burn within that which is not in agreement with God or His purpose for us, so that the impurities of our character are replaced with godly characteristics that were not there before (Revelation 3:18). "These things saith the Son of God, who hath his eyes like unto a flame of fire" (Revelation 2:18 KJV). "That the genuineness of your faith, being much more precious than gold that perishes, though it is tested by fire, may be found to praise, honor, and glory at the revelation of Jesus Christ" (1 Peter 1:7 NKJV).

The apostle Peter writes that the testing of your faith is more precious than gold, and he and James both say that there is something to find after the successful navigation of the test. "Blessed is the man who endures temptation; for when he has been approved, he will receive the crown of life which the Lord has promised to those who love Him" (James 1:12 NKJV).

Jesus had to endure temptation and testing in the wilderness. The Holy Spirit led Jesus into the wilderness (God's will for Him) to be tempted by the Devil. This was recorded when Jesus entered His earthly ministry, and His success in this test propelled Him into the purpose of the Father for His coming. If Jesus had avoided this time of testing, great loss would have resulted for Him and for all humanity.

There were many men and women in the Bible who were tested—Abraham, Job, Joseph, Hosea, and Deborah, to mention a few from the Old Testament. The early church in Acts also endured numerous tests, not to mention the many men and women throughout church history. Today many Christians try to avoid such trials by listening to preachers who tell them pleasant things that are palatable but neglectful of the true gospel. "For the time will come when men will not put up with sound doctrine. Instead, to suit their own desires, they will gather around them a great number of teachers to say what their itching ears want to hear" (2 Timothy 4:3 NIV).

If we are to have better Christians—and we do need men and women of character—then the Lord must try the metal of their lives so that they can be entrusted with the true gospel. Testing will be the basis to prove genuine faith and character. "But as we have been approved by God to be entrusted with the gospel, even so we speak, not as pleasing men, but God who tests our hearts" (1 Thessalonians 2:4 NKJV).

Consider this as well: "Test me, O Lord, and try me, examine my heart and my mind" (Psalm 26:2 NIV).

The Lord took us from who we were to what we are, and He will take us to what we will become. So if we encounter suffering or testing, we need to willingly surrender to the Lord and allow Him to change us into what He wants us to become. Jesus is our example. Even He had to submit to His Father's will.

CHAPTER 5

THE GREAT SPOILER

The Bible refers to Satan, the one who opposes all that is good and all that comes from God. He is the adversary of God and man. He steals, kills, and destroys anyone and anything he can, and he brings great ruin upon mankind. Even though Satan can do great damage to the Christian, we give him too much credit for being the main source of the problems Christians have. God has limited his power and the scope of his influence, and the Christian who is walking in the Spirit does not need to fret over him. Satan does not have control over those who walk with God because Christ is our hiding place. "You are my hiding place; You shall preserve me from trouble; You shall surround me with songs of deliverance" (Psalm 32:7 NKJV).

The believer should keep his attention upon the Lord, walk with Him, and not be overly concerned with Satan because Satan does not control his life. What does not get enough attention is one of the great hindrances to the Christian—the flesh!

What is the flesh, and what does this word mean in the Bible? There are different usages of the word, and the context determines the meaning in the verse. The word *flesh* is used to identify the flesh of man, animals, fish, and birds. It refers to the physical life, which was created by God to exist on the physical level, and in that context it does not carry any negative connotation—that is, unless the body is used to express the sins of a carnal nature.

The flesh also refers to the worldly, human nature with its passions and appetites, human reasoning, lusts, the unregenerate nature of man, and the seat of sin in man. This is the area that causes so many problems for man and spoils his relationship with God. The desires and appetites of the carnal nature will lead to sin, which brings separation from God. Some Christians say they have difficulty discerning when they are moving in the flesh, but to those who want to know, it should not be hard to recognize the difference.

Worldliness

Consider the following passages: "The first man [was] from out of earth, made of dust" (1 Corinthians 15:47a AMP). (The first man refers to Adam.) "Now those who are made of the dust are like him, who was first made of the dust" (1 Corinthians 15:48a AMP).

Because man is of the earth, there is a tie between his heart and the world. That is why there is a draw toward the world and toward worldly thinking and to all that the world has to offer. That which is of the world—fame, success, honor, wealth, selfishness, greed, ambition, pride, and reputation—has its draw upon the heart of man, calling him to a life consumed with self-pursuits and a life that is moving toward ruin. The web is spun. The trap is set, waiting for the unsuspecting to fall in and be killed by their own desires and pursuits, and so another victim has been caught up in the world system! Those who have not experienced the salvation of Jesus Christ are in bondage to the sin that keeps them attached to that which is worldly. But the Christian should have escaped the corruption in the world caused by evil desires and should be living above the world.

We see worldly Christians who can hardly be distinguished from those in the world around them. They act like the world, talk like the world, think like the world, and are involved with some of the same activities worldly people are, and in a group you would not even know that they were Christians. Rather than being separate from the world, they conform to the world. Jesus said of His true followers, "They are not of the world, even as I am not of the world" (John 17:14 KJV).

The Apostle Paul said, "What communion hath light with darkness?" (2 Corinthians 6:14 KJV). Consider the following as well: "Therefore Come out from among them and be separate, says the Lord. Do not touch what is unclean, and I will receive you" (2 Corinthians 6:17 NKJV). "Be not conformed to this world" (Romans 12:2 KJV).

To be conformed is to form or mold one's behavior in accordance with a particular pattern or set of standards, to shape one's behavior, to conform one's life (Louw, 1996).

In their hearts the believers are to be set apart from the world and not conformed to its many influences. If there is a heart that wants to see, the Holy Spirit will bring illumination so that he or she will be able to distinguish what is worldly from what is not. The Lord will work within to bring about the separation needed so that the draw of the world no longer has the effect it once did. Now the choice comes— whether one wants Jesus or wants to compromise and choose what the world has to offer.

Carnal Reasoning

God has given to man a wonderful gift that separates him from the animal kingdom, and that is the ability to reason. The animals do not reason like man but function according to instinct. Reasoning and having one's mind form thoughts is not a bad thing, but we must realize that earthly reasoning, when it comes to the things of God, will most likely take one in the wrong direction. "[That is] because the mind of the flesh [with its carnal thoughts and purposes] is hostile to God, for it does not submit itself to God's Law; indeed, it cannot" (Romans 8:7 AMP).

Our thoughts can be influenced by Satan, causing extreme blindness to the point that Christians may not even know that they are blind in certain areas of their lives. Decisions made in that condition will result in lives that are lived not knowing the true will of God. There must be a willingness and dependency upon God to shine light into the darkness (the blindness) and to give us the opportunity to make correct judgments based upon what the Word of God reveals.

The apostle Paul wrote to the church in Corinth and said that they were carnal Christians. Being carnal implied that they were viewing things, to some degree, similar to the way the rest of the world was. And because the Corinthian Christians were carnal, they were limited as to what the Lord could reveal to them through the Apostle Paul.

> And I, brethren, could not speak to you as to spiritual people but as to carnal, as to babes in Christ. I fed you with milk and not with solid food; for until now you were not able to receive it, and even now you are still not able; for you are still carnal. For where there are envy, strife, and divisions among you, are you not carnal and behaving like mere men? (1 Corinthians 3:1–3 NKJV)

Because of the carnality of the Corinthian church, they limited what the Lord wanted to give them. The Lord can send a preacher with a message for a church, and because of the carnality in the church that person can be rejected or misunderstood. We normally do not think that carnality brings great limitations, but that which the Lord desires to do in the believer is thwarted until his or her carnality can be destroyed.

The Christian man who gravitates toward listening to his own thoughts (Isaiah 65:2) instead of God's Word can find himself in a precarious position. His own thoughts can get him into trouble by leading him in a direction contrary to the ways of God. This is common with those who have not had their minds renewed. A renewed mind is a mind made new by the Word of God and not by Christian music, testimonies, activities, talks about the Lord, or any other means the church may think will accomplish this. "And be not conformed to this world: but be ye transformed by the renewing of your mind" (Romans 12:2 KJV).

The Lord says, "For My thoughts are not your thoughts," but that does not mean that He does not want our thoughts to be like His. The

Holy Spirit will work in the heart of the Christian man to begin the process of changing his thinking so that his thoughts start to reflect the Lord's. This is a very slow and at times very difficult process because of ingrained carnal reasoning. Because of the tendency to hold on to that reasoning, it takes time to bring about the change the Lord desires. The carnal mind is the enemy of God because it resists the change that could bring the Christian into agreement with the thoughts of God. The carnal mind does not want to give up any ground that it has, and it will fight like the Philistines fought when Israel tried to advance. "That he might sanctify and cleanse her with the washing of water by the word" (Ephesians 5:26 NKJV).

We can find in the Bible different washings with specific purposes:

- the washing of the sacrifice (Leviticus 1:13)
- the washing or purification of the priests for service (Leviticus 16:4; Exodus 30:18–19)
- the washing of regeneration (Titus 3:5)
- cleansing by the blood (1 John 1:7)
- cleansing by faith (Acts 15:8–9)
- self-cleansing (2 Corinthians 7:1; James 4:8)
- cleansing of the Christian from unrighteousness (1 John 1:9)

The Bible also speaks of "the washing of water by the Word," a phrase we see in Ephesians 5:26. This washing is very important for the Christian and is necessary to make a separation between the person's thinking and the thinking of the world. The Lord is faithful to send His Word and bring about a change in one's thinking, actions, carnal desires, direction and in whatever way He sees is necessary and beneficial. God's Word has a bathing influence on the receiving heart and can clean the heart in ways like nothing else can.

Lust

Lust in the Bible means "desire, longing, craving." Desires fall into one of two areas. There are godly desires—those that move toward the Lord, His Word, and His will and those that the Holy Spirit births to accomplish His purpose. Jesus desired to eat the Passover with His apostles before He suffered. Paul desired the spiritual welfare of the churches. These are godly desires birthed within by the Holy Spirit to a spiritual end.

Jesus said of the Comforter that He would testify of Him or that the Holy Spirit would try to create a desire for Jesus in our hearts. That is quite a job, considering all of the distractions in the world and all the things that clamor for the heart's attention. There are as many desires in the heart of man as there are things in the world. So the Holy Spirit will work on our behalf to bring separation from the world so that our desire will be Jesus.

Then there are desires that come forth from the lower nature, desires that focus upon the self-centered nature of man and the sinful nature of Adam that we were born with. The longings and cravings of the carnal, sinful nature are powerful and will take man further and further away from God.

The Bible shows some of the results of evil desires that people can have. One of the more destructive desires not understood or seen by many is the desire to be rich. "But those who desire to be rich fall into temptation and a snare, and into many foolish and harmful lusts which drown men in destruction and perdition" (1 Timothy 6:9 NKJV). "No one can serve two masters; for either he will hate the one and love the other, or he will stand by and be devoted to the one and despise and be against the other. You cannot serve God and mammon (deceitful riches, money, possessions, or whatever is trusted in" (Matthew 6:24 AMP).

The allurements of the world are very powerful because they touch something deep within man. There is an attraction that beckons to the very nature of mankind and cannot be successfully denied apart from a work of the Holy Spirit within. When one hears the Word of God and has desires for other things, the Word of God is choked and never produces fruit. In the book of James it says that evil desires warring within were causing the quarrels in the church. The cravings of the sinful nature will try to bring about the fulfillment of some ungodly desire, which is not of the Father but is of the world. These fleshly lusts war against the soul and bring about destruction in the life of those who surrender to them. If lust continues, it will produce works, and those works will be manifest. "Now the works of the flesh are evident, which are: adultery, fornication, uncleanness, lewdness, idolatry, sorcery, hatred, contentions, jealousies, outbursts of wrath, selfish ambitions" (Galatians 5:19–20 NKJV). Consider the following passages as well: "For all that is in the world—the lust of the flesh, the lust of the eyes, and the pride of life—is not of the Father but is of the world" (1 John 2:16 NKJV). "Beloved, I beg you as sojourners and pilgrims, abstain from fleshly lusts which war against the soul" (1 Peter 2:11 NKJV).

There is a war waged against the souls of Christians who want to walk with God. The weapons used include "all that is in the world" (1 John 2:16), and they are used to try to touch your fleshly nature and make your life ineffective.

There are various characteristics of the flesh mentioned in the scriptures, some of which include the following:

- indulging sinful passions (desires) (Romans 7:5)
- setting the mind on the things that satisfy the flesh (Romans 8:5)
- fulfilling the evil cravings of the physical nature (Romans 13:14)
- being self-willed and self-loving (2 Peter 2:10)
- bringing no profit at all (John 6:63)

The desires of the Holy Spirit are quite different from the desires of the flesh. The Holy Spirit longs to lead the believer away from the destruction the flesh brings, so that spiritual life and character result:

- be holy for the Lord is holy (1 Peter 1:16)
- setting the mind above (Colossians 3:2)

- desiring what is contrary to the sinful nature (Galatians 5:17)
- being others centered (Matthew 18:11; John 13:4–5)
- being profitable (1 Timothy 6:6)

Fleshly desires war against the soul, and the Holy Spirit wars against the flesh. The Christian cannot walk after the flesh and after the Spirit. He will live in one place or the other.

The Flesh Brings Death

In the epistle of James it states a process that starts with lust and ends in a place that the person does not expect. "Then, when desire has conceived, it gives birth to sin; and sin, when it is full-grown, brings forth death" (James 1:15 NKJV). This verse progresses in the following way:

1) Desire—the desire or lust for that which is not given by God but is taken by man. Genesis 3:6 says, "She (Eve) took" and "her husband (Adam) ate."
2) Sin—is that which God forbids because it causes separation from Him. Sin misses the mark that would have brought spiritual life and health, but instead it causes death.
3) Death—the result of ungodly lusts and desires. The lust that was hiding in the heart is manifest through the death it brings.

"For when we were in the flesh, the motions of sins, which were by the law, did work in our members to bring forth fruit unto death" (Romans 7:5 KJV).

Remember that when lust begins, it takes time before the resulting death occurs. This is not necessarily talking about physical death but spiritual death, which separates one from God and causes the Christian to miss the will and purpose of the Lord for his or her life. Ungodly lusts, passions, and affections all originate in the flesh. All evil inclinations move from the flesh and will affect every area of one's life. The flesh motivates men to pursue lives that practice the acts of the sinful nature—sexual immorality, impurity, idolatry, hatred, jealousy, etc. This cannot be avoided unless the flesh with all of its passions and desires is crucified—that is, put to death (Galatians 5:24). Those who are Christ's are to have crucified the appetites and desires of the fleshly, sinful nature and consider them dead with Christ on the cross, no longer allowing them to have power over their lives.

The apostle Paul writes to the Corinthian church and calls them carnal.

> HOWEVER, BRETHREN, I could not talk to you as to spiritual [men], but as to nonspiritual [men of the flesh, in whom the carnal nature predominates], as to mere infants [in the new life] in Christ [unable to talk yet!] I fed you with milk, not solid food, for you were not yet strong enough [to be ready for it]; but even yet you are not strong enough [to be ready for it], For you are still [unspiritual, having the nature] of the flesh [under the control of ordinary impulses]. For as long as [there are] envying and jealousy and wrangling and factions among you, are you not unspiritual and of the flesh, behaving yourselves after a human standard and like mere (unchanged) men? (1 Corinthians 3:1–3 AMP)

The Corinthian church was under the influence of their carnal cravings, and because of that, they could not advance past being babes in Christ. Even though Paul had great wealth to give them, they could not receive it.

Likewise it is possible today that churches can be as carnal as the Corinthians and not view themselves as such. In Revelation, Jesus told the pastor and the church of the Laodiceans, about how they were poor when they thought they were rich. Our perspective of our spiritual condition can be much different than the Lord's. We can be carnal and think we are spiritual, so we should not think more highly of ourselves than we should, and we should look to the Lord to reveal our true spiritual condition. "So then they that are in the flesh cannot please God" (Romans 8:8 KJV).

Those who are in the flesh are not able to please God. No matter how much one goes to church, reads the Bible, prays, or does good things, if the flesh nature in the person is alive, he or she cannot please God. "If we live in the Spirit, let us also walk in the Spirit" (Galatians 5:25 KJV).

The one who lives and walks in the Spirit can only be one who has crucified the flesh. That man has allowed his fleshly desires to die! This death defines those who are in the relationship that Christ desires (Galatians 5:24).

The flesh has many destructive qualities that men do not recognize as destructive, including some of the following:

- Self-will: With the Israelites in the wilderness we can see their stubborn attitude toward Moses. With some Christians it is characterized by the pursuit of one's own wishes and direction. Those who choose their own will over the will of God for them are self-willed.
- Self-centeredness: This involves being engrossed in self and being concerned with one's own desires and needs, and is visible in egotistic behavior and preoccupation with self.
- Self-strength: This would be the dependence upon one's strength and ability apart from and independent of the Lord. This would include mental reasoning and the strength to be self-reliant, self-ruling, self-supporting, and unconnected to Jesus.
- Self-desires: Within an individual there are longings for what he or she wants. The person sees a hope for what pleases him or her and inner movement toward the object of one's desire.
- Selfish ways: Moving in selfish ways is the course that one charts who is apart from God's will, and that pursuit ends in spiritual ruin now and in the future. Selfish ways are also

habitual manners that originate within the carnal nature that goes contrary to the ways of God.

- Self-direction: This is the reliance upon self to direct one's life according to natural reasoning, which has some goal or purpose that seems to have temporary benefit to the individual.
- Self-made: Being self-made is the culmination of many self-born decisions that direct one down a road with a very different outcome than if the Lord was in control. A self-made Christian will have the desire for others to hear or see them as being a great man or woman of God. This is flesh and not recognized by many. But the Christian who does not love publicity, does not have the desire for reputation, and is not interested in gathering people to him or herself is one who is not moved by or controlled by the flesh and has no desire to be self-made!

The carnal, fleshly Christian will see nothing wrong with some of these things, accepting them as parts of life. But those who are not blinded by the flesh will understand that their lives are not about these ambitions.

It is not difficult to see that the flesh is destructive. The flesh is the enemy of spiritual maturity and is a roadblock to experiencing the depths of God. The great spoiler, the flesh, has hindered many Christians from receiving their full inheritance, and it will disqualify them for the marriage to the Lord.

In Leviticus the flesh of the offering had to be burnt with fire on the third day (Leviticus 7:17–18; 19:6–7). The third day is representative of the resurrection life, and that is *when the flesh is destroyed*. When the flesh is destroyed within the Christian, he will be prepared for the marriage!

Jesus will not marry flesh! The bride must make herself ready!

CHAPTER 6

DEDICATION

Most people today do not take the time to examine their lives and hearts to see what direction they are going, and they never question where that direction will lead them. There are not many Christians who examine themselves to see if their lives are meaningful in the eyes of the Lord. Nor is there concern to develop the character of Jesus within them. In their thinking, it is enough to get to heaven, and that becomes their main focus.

There is a deeper walk waiting for the Christian, but to experience it, the person's heart must point toward the Lord. "I have set the Lord always before me" (Psalm 16:8 KJV).

This statement by David shows the spiritual posture of his heart—that it was poised toward the Lord. The Christian is to come out from among the world and be separate, and the believer is not to touch the unclean thing. This does not necessarily mean a physical touching, but it can reference that which is touched with our heart. We may not touch some unclean thing with our hands and yet touch it with our hearts (Matthew 5:28). Separation is to be first internal and then external as the Spirit leads. We are to separate for the purpose of God and have hearts that are willing to follow on to know the Lord.

What is the focus of our hearts? This is a sobering question, and how we answer can be even more sobering! It may come as a surprise to some that every single person has some focus in life, be it self-centered or God-centered. The focus of our hearts will strongly determine where we are and where we are going. For example, if sports are the focus of the heart, then sports will influence what one does and what one considers important. If music is the focus, then the heart will move in that direction.

There are many things in the world that can demand the attention of the heart, so many that they could not be listed, and the focus of one's heart can change from time to time. Many times what has the attention of the heart comes out when he or she opens their mouth. We then get a glimpse into what the individual holds at the center of their life.

When someone or something other than Jesus has the attention of Christians, the commitment that the Lord desires from them will be lacking. The enemy of our souls, Satan, will place before the Christian many things to try to disrupt the focus of his or her heart. In this life there are many hindrances that are encountered, designed to subtly direct us away into a place where life has no meaning and little or nothing of spiritual value is produced.

The main distractions that Christians experience include the difficulties of life. No one living in this world can escape difficulties. We all will go through many different circumstances, some good and some seemingly very bad. If we truly love God, He will see to it that every circumstance will work together for our good, whether we see the good or not, because God is in control. We may even say, "How can the Lord use this horrendous situation for any good?" But remember that our vision of the ways of God is very limited. We cannot see the beginning from the end. "Where were you when I laid the foundations of the earth? Tell Me, if you have understanding" (Job 38:4 NKJV).

Every man born into this earth is in his own unique circumstance that in many instances he believes no one understands or endures like he does. The one who has been a Christian for a while should have learned some things about circumstances.

Circumstances are almost always temporary. The circumstances you find yourself in today will probably change in the future. We endure some circumstances for a short time. Some last longer, and others drag on for many years. Remember, however, that they will all end someday.

Our personal circumstances will cry as a persistent crowd of people in order to get our undivided attention. This is a constant with everyone, and we should expect to hear this cry. It will not be external but instead internal. The outcry of the heart will get louder and louder until it drowns out the Lord, the one who is to be the focus of our hearts. It is very important to see and understand this because it will help us to redirect our hearts to Him. It may be quite a struggle to turn a deaf ear to our circumstances, not allowing them to control us, and to look to Jesus in the midst of the clamor and hear Him. He is the one who can work all things for our good, even though we may believe that that is impossible. Jesus, who upholds all things by the Word of His power, can work all things for our good regardless of how bad a circumstance appears. The key for the Christian is to focus on the Lord and not on the circumstance, which will require the exercising of the heart.

How we view the Lord and our circumstances is very important because it affects what God can reveal to us in and through them. In the book of Psalms, we read something very enlightening about Moses and the Israelites. "He made known his ways unto Moses, His acts unto the children of Israel" (Psalm 103:7 KJV).

Moses and the Israelites were in the same circumstances in the wilderness. The playing field was level, and what made the difference was their hearts. Moses, Joshua, and Caleb viewed the Lord and the circumstance differently than the rest of the people did. Joshua and Caleb said, "Let us go up at once and take possession, for we are well able to overcome it," while the others said, "We are not able to go up against the people, for they are stronger than we. And they gave the children of Israel a bad report of the land" (Numbers 13:30–32 NKJV). They were in the same situation but with different hearts. Someone once said that circumstances would either make us bitter or better, depending upon how we react to them.

Joshua and Caleb had a different view of God and a different view of their circumstance, which enabled them to navigate through their situation and come out successfully. In the wilderness circumstances

Moses learned the ways of God, but the other Israelites only saw the acts (miracles) and never really saw the Lord.

The circumstances that the Christian finds him or herself in can provide the breeding ground for a deeper spiritual life in Christ. They become the stage that the Lord uses to reveal His will and His ways in a very personal way. Jesus can produce His likeness in the cooperating heart and can do what would be impossible apart from those particular circumstances. We can abhor the situation, and yet the surrendered hearts will learn and grow in unimaginable ways because the Lord is at work in them. Jesus is able to mold you in His hands as clay and form your life into what would be impossible if you would try to control your own circumstances. So present to God your body as a living sacrifice. Relinquish control, agree with Him in His personal dealings with you, and be dedicated to God.

Will we succumb to our difficulties and never progress in our growth? Will we fail and wander around for forty years in a spiritual wilderness like the Israelites did in their wilderness? It does not have to be so. We do not have to go through the same situations over and over again. In Revelation, Jesus addresses the seven churches, and there is something that He says to each of them. He said to each church, "To him who overcomes I will—" Each church found themselves in a different situation. Nevertheless, Jesus said that they needed to be overcomers. Our difficulties are to make us overcomers in Christ not because we confess some scripture but because He has given us victory in the situation that we are living in. The circumstances do not have to change for us to experience victory in them. We must look to Jesus in the midst of life's troubles and allow Him to do something within us that causes us to see Him and the situations in the light of eternity. This can be quite a work of the Holy Spirit, one that we will recognize as being of Him and not of us.

One of the things that Moses, Joshua, and Caleb had in common was a strong dedication to the Lord. For the Christian to walk closely to God, the believer will have to be committed to Him no matter what the personal circumstance may be. What are we dedicated to? Are we dedicated to the Lord?

Without strong dedication to the Lord, we will not be interested in gleaning spiritual things from Him in our circumstances. We will only be interested in changing them because they are unpleasant. If that is the case, we will miss opportunity after opportunity to be conformed to the image of Jesus Christ and will pass from this life with great loss.

The Bible has quite a lot to say about dedication. In the Old Testament, we read about the consecration of the priests in order for them to serve the Lord in the tabernacle. There are other examples of dedicated people, such as Moses, Joshua, Esther, the judges, seers, prophets, apostles, etc. But there is a New Testament Greek word used to embody the central meaning of the word *dedication*, and that word is *agape*.

The English word *love* is used to translate the Greek word *agape*. The word *love* is a very broad term that does not accurately portray the word used in the Greek. From the English word *love*, various meanings can be intended. For example, we could mean the love of God toward us, our love for God, the love for a spouse, a love for a child or parent, love toward others, love toward the world, love toward food or some other pleasure, or the score in a tennis game. The word itself does not give any specifics that give the reader an accurate meaning. But in the Greek there are different words used that are translated as love, each of which narrows down the thought that is trying to be portrayed. The Greek has different words that describe various types of love, such as *eros*, *philia*, and agape.

Agape is the most common Greek meaning used for the word *love* in the Bible, and it is the most familiar to Christians. It is understood by most Christians as heartfelt feeling and affection or unconditional love, but the English word that best describes agape is dedication. In the scriptures there are certain characteristics in the usage of the word *agape* that can help us understand what this word really means.

Two of the main characteristics seen with this word include dedication and sacrifice. To illustrate this, these words are inserted in the following scriptures: "For God so loved (*agapao*, meaning "was dedicated to") the world that He gave His only begotten Son, that whoever believes in Him should not perish but have everlasting life" (John 3:16 NKJV). The Father was so *dedicated* to the world that He sent Jesus.

"For God so loved (*agapao*, meaning "sacrificed for") the world, that He gave His only begotten Son, that whoever believes in Him should not perish, but have everlasting life" (John 3:16 NKJV). There was a *sacrifice* made by the Father to send Jesus to die.

"But God demonstrates His own love (agape, meaning dedication and sacrifice) toward us, in that while we were still sinners, Christ died for us" (Romans 5:8 NKJV).

"In this the love (agape, meaning dedication and sacrifice) of God was manifested toward us, that God has sent His only begotten Son into the world, that we might live through Him" (1 John 4:9 NKJV). The Father demonstrated His *dedication* toward us. The *sacrifice* of the Father and Jesus were manifest to all of us.

It is not difficult to see the dedication of the Father and Jesus toward humanity and specifically to the Christian. This love (agape in reference to dedication) we receive at physical birth, and so is that ability to dedicate our lives to whatever is within our hearts. With this love, we make decisions that determine the direction of this love, whether it will become God-centered or self-centered. With our will we determine the direction that love (agape) travels, or we could say that we decide where that love goes. "Woe unto you, Pharisees! for ye love (agapao) the uppermost seats in the synagogues, and greetings in the markets" (Luke 11:43 KJV).

The Pharisees, who were not saved, had this agape, and they decided to direct it toward their desire for the uppermost seats in the synagogues. Their dedication was not toward the Lord. It was not God-centered. Rather it was self-centered and self-seeking. "You shall love (*agapao*, meaning "be dedicated to") the Lord your God with all your heart, and with all your soul, and with all your mind" (Matthew 22:37 NKJV).

One of the reasons the Lord says this is because man can love (be dedicated to) so many other things.

Consider the following: "We love (agapao) Him because He first loved us" (1 John 4:19 NKJV). "So husbands ought to love (agapao) their own wives as their own bodies" (Ephesians 5:28 NKJV). In these scriptures we are to love or be dedicated to the Lord God, and men are to be dedicated to their wives. This becomes the choice of the individual Christian.

It becomes a very sobering thought to understand that God has given us a free will so that we can choose the direction not only of our lives but of the love (agape) that God has given to us to accomplish either a selfish or godly purpose!

What do we as Christians love, or to what are we dedicated? We can be dedicated to sports, TV, reading, work, the pursuit of money, pornography, drugs, alcohol, news, success, knowledge, gossip, crafts, hobbies, etc. We can direct this love toward just about anything, and man can take something that God has intended for good and make it evil. It is sad to see Christians share some of the same pursuits as the world from which they are to separate. Because we have been born from above, we have a great advantage in that we have the Holy Spirit, who brings illumination, alerting us to the direction of our hearts. After we see this, we can direct agape in the correct way to accomplish the purpose of God through our lives.

What is the focus of our hearts? As we grow and mature as Christians, the Lord should have worked on us to sever many of the things that have held our attention, replacing them with the pursuit of God, which we may not have had early in our walk. Our attention may have been on works, knowledge, understanding, or any number of things we mistakenly thought was our target. But He alone is to be the focal point. He alone is worthy of our dedication.

Dedication is very important in order for us to obtain what the Lord provides for us. We experience birth into the kingdom, but we are to go forward to obtain what awaits us in the kingdom. The Lord gave the Promised Land to the Israelites, but under the leadership of Joshua, they had to go forward to obtain what the Lord had provided for them.

There are kingdom principles listed below that the Christian is to be functioning in, and there are kingdom characteristics that are to be within. Some of these kingdom principles are the following:

If you want to live, you must die.
"He who finds his life will lose it, and he who loses his life for My sake will find it" (Matthew 10:39 NKJV).

The way down is the way up.
"For whoever exalts himself will be humbled, and he who humbles himself will be exalted" (Luke 14:11 NKJV).

Death will bring life.
"Most assuredly, I say to you, unless a grain of wheat falls into the ground and dies, it remains alone; but if it dies, it produces much grain. He who loves his life will lose it, and he who hates his life in this world will keep it for eternal life" (John 12:24–25 NKJV).

Loss is gain.
"But what things were gain to me, these I have counted loss for Christ. Yet indeed I also count all things loss for the excellence of the knowledge of Christ Jesus my Lord, for whom I have suffered the loss of all things, and count them as rubbish, that I may gain Christ" (Philippians 3:7–8 NKJV).

To become rich, you must become poor.
"For you know the grace of our Lord Jesus Christ, that though He was rich, yet for your sakes He became poor, that you through His poverty might become rich" (2 Corinthians 8:9 NKJV).

Not all Christians are functioning in these principles, even though God provided these maxims to them. It will take dedication to the kingdom of God to obtain what is in the kingdom. "But seek the kingdom of God, and all these things shall be added to you" (Luke 12:31 NKJV).

In the previous verse Jesus says to seek, which in the Greek is a command to seek in order to find. What are we to find? We are to find what Jesus has appointed for us in the kingdom. Without an overwhelming dedication to the kingdom, there will be the loss of what could have been found and a failure to have these kingdom principles at work in one's life.

Kingdom principles begin to operate when there is true surrender, walking with God, and a pursuit of God moving within.

Some *kingdom characteristics* found in the parables that Jesus taught concerning the kingdom are:

Parable	Characteristic
Mustard seed (least of seeds)	Spiritual growth that benefits others (Mark 4:30–32)
Leaven	A type of the gospel of the kingdom that is to spread in one's life (Luke 13:20–21)
Hidden treasure	Whatever the price, the kingdom is worth it (Matthew 13:44)
Householder (landowner)	Heart condition that determines first and last (Matthew 20:1–16)
Marriage of king's son	Heart response (Matthew 22:1–14)
King taking account of his servants	Compassion and forgiveness (Matthew 18:21–35)

These characteristics are to be in the Christian through the work of God in his or her life. If there has been cooperation with the Holy Spirit in His specific personal dealings, then these virtues will begin to develop and grow within. This is another example of how the Lord prepares the Christian to become the bride.

The importance of dedication cannot be overstated. Too much is at stake. One's dedication strongly determines what a person carries with them after this life. The Lord has supplied all that we need in order to give to Him the dedication that He desires and what we need to bring us to completion. Without dedication to Him, the preparation of the Christian will lack because their attention was on something other than Jesus, and the resulting work remained unfinished.

CHAPTER 7

QUALIFICATIONS

There are verses in the Bible that Christians use to assert what they believe that the Bible says pertaining to them. Because they have received Christ as their Savior they may have confessed or claimed certain verses. Are there promises in the Bible that require meeting certain standards to bring about the desired fulfillment promised? Or is being saved all that is necessary to lay claim to the scriptures? Does the Christian have to confess and believe to make them come to pass? To answer these questions, we must look closely at various scriptures. It is prudent to make a careful examination of the verse to see if there are any qualifying factors involved.

Required Conditions

God said to Abraham, "To your descendants I have given this land" (Genesis 15:18 NKJV). In Exodus 3:8, the Lord gave two reasons why He came down to the Israelites in Egypt. It was to deliver the Israelites from Egypt and to take them to the Promised Land. In Exodus, the Lord also says that He would bring them into the land that He was giving them, and He told them to search it out. From the statements concerning the Israelites and the Promised Land, it would seem that it was a sure thing that they would go in and possess the land. But we know that the generation that came out of Egypt did not enter. Why? In different places in the Bible we read reasons why they did not enter.

In Numbers, ten of the twelve spies brought back an evil report, which the people believed, disqualifying them from the blessing of God. God said that these Israelites would not see the land. Not only their unbelief but also their rebellion prohibited them from entry. Even though God had given them the land, they had to meet certain conditions for that to come to pass.

> When your fathers tempted me, proved me, and saw my work. Forty years long was I grieved with this generation, and said, It is a people that do err in their heart, and they have not known my ways: Unto whom I sware in my wrath that they should not enter into my rest. (Psalms 95:9–11 KJV)

You may also consider the following: "So we see that they could not enter in because of unbelief" (Hebrews 3:19 KJV).

Because of the rebellious nature of these Israelites, God was not able to bring them into the Promised Land. They did not qualify for the blessing that was prepared for them. Even though the promise of entering the Promised Land was given to them, conditions had to be fulfilled for them to qualify to go in and possess the land.

Some other examples of qualifying include the following:

1) Isaac and Rebecca had two sons, Esau and Jacob. Esau was the firstborn, and because he was, he had all the rights of the birthright. Esau despised his birthright, and because he was hungry, he gave it up to Jacob for bread and stew (Genesis 25:33–34). He disqualified himself for that position, and even though he was an heir to the birthright, he never inherited the double portion and all the allotted blessings associated with being the firstborn.

2) In 1 Peter 2:9, we read that we are a peculiar people, a special people. The use of this phrase is in Exodus 19 and in Deuteronomy 14 and 26. To be a peculiar (special) people is

not automatic, but it does require obedience. In Titus 2:14, the setting for being a peculiar people is that the Lord might purify for Himself a special people. Christians may say and believe they are a special people, but the conditions are obedience and purity. "Now therefore, if you will indeed obey My voice and keep My covenant, then you shall be a special treasure to Me above all people" (Exodus 19:5 NKJV).

3) King Solomon had placed a heavy burden of taxation upon the people to finish building the temple. There was a king named Rehoboam, the son of Solomon, who, after the death of Solomon, increased the burden of taxes on the people. The people rebelled against Rehoboam because of this heavy yoke, and they chose Jeroboam to lead the tribes that broke away. The Lord used a prophet to tell Jeroboam that the Lord would be with him and would build for him an enduring house as He built for David. The condition that Jeroboam had to meet was to take heed to do all that the Lord had commanded, to walk in His ways, and to do what is right in the sight of the Lord (1 Kings 11:38). This promise was unfulfilled in Jeroboam's life because he did not satisfy the conditions.

4) The Lord told the second generation of Israelites who came out of Egypt to go in and possess the land. Before they could possess, they had to dispossess and destroy the inhabitants. Without doing exactly what the Lord told them, they would never have been able to possess the land, even though it was the promise of the Lord to them.

5) In Titus 1:7–9 and 1 Timothy 3:2–7, we clearly see that there are qualifications for an overseer. The main thought in these verses is that not everyone qualifies in a position of leadership. Because a person has experienced salvation does not necessarily equip him or her to be an overseer. One must meet certain conditions for that office. If qualifications are necessary in the church here on earth, what makes Christians think that it will not be so after we leave this life?

It does not matter how much one speaks the Word or confesses their faith. If one does not meet the conditions, it will be an exercise in futility. A Christian can confess and believe a scripture with all their heart and strength, but the danger is that it can lead to striving. Christians must understand that the Lord desires fulfillment in His people. He wants to see everyone obtain the promises, but we must examine the scriptures closely to see what condition or conditions are set forth that are necessary to bring about the fulfillment of a promise. Some sample scriptures that clearly show the attached condition are as follows:

> "If you are willing and obedient, you shall eat the good of the land" (Isaiah 1:19 NKJV). To eat of the good land, one must be willing and obedient.

> "Heirs of God and joint heirs with Christ, if indeed we suffer with Him" (Romans 8:17 NKJV). Being an heir and joint heir will require from us some suffering.

> "You will keep him in perfect peace, whose mind is stayed on You, Because he trusts in You" (Isaiah 26:3 NKJV). Perfect peace comes through trusting in the Lord and having the mind steadfast on Him.

> "But if you are led by the Spirit, you are not under the law" (Galatians 5:18 NKJV). The stipulation for not being under the law is that we are under the leading the Spirit. Meeting this condition is necessary and will be a learning process.

> "He shall be like a tree planted by the rivers of water, That brings forth its fruit in its season, whose leaf also shall not wither; and whatever he does shall prosper" (Psalm 1:3 NKJV). In this context, to bring forth fruit

and to prosper, one must look at the conditions found in verses 1 and 2. They are not to walk in the council of the ungodly or stand in the path of sinners or sit in the seat of the scornful but rather meditate in the law of the Lord day and night.

"Humble yourselves therefore under the mighty hand of God, that He may exalt you in due time" (1 Peter 5:6 KJV). The Lord will exalt the Christian, but the person must humble him or herself. There is no other way up than the way down!

"Delight yourself also in the Lord, And He shall give you the desires of your heart" (Psalm 37:4 NKJV). For the Lord to give the desires of the heart, it will take a soft pliable heart, which results in our desires being like His.

"Blessed is the man who perseveres under trial, because when he has stood the test, he will receive the crown of life that God has promised to those who love Him" (James 1:12 NIV). To receive this particular crown, successful endurance in the trial is necessary. The promise of the crown of life is to those who truly love the Lord. Jesus said that if you truly love Him, you would keep His commandments.

Many Christians live their lives as if no qualifications exist concerning the scriptures! They may believe what a preacher says rather than examining the verses for themselves. Confession does not bring possession. Rather meeting the conditions will bring possession!

The Ten Virgins

In Matthew 25, Jesus likened the kingdom of God to ten virgins that took their lamps and went out to meet the bridegroom. In this parable there were five wise and five foolish virgins. The wise took enough oil for their lamps, and the five foolish virgins did not take enough oil with them.

At midnight the bridegroom came, and all the virgins trimmed their lamps. This indicates that they lit all their lamps, but only the five wise virgins had extra oil. Typically oil in the Bible represents the Holy Spirit. The extra oil can refer to the work of the Holy Spirit to keep one in the arrangements of God, designed to bring the Christian to the place where he or she is prepared for the greater purpose, namely the union with Christ.

The five foolish virgins were not prepared because they were not willing to go through the things that would bring about preparedness in their lives. The attitude of the virgins toward obtaining oil beforehand was what made them either wise or foolish. So the foolish virgins asked the wise virgins for oil. They responded, "No, lest there should not be enough for us and you; but go rather to those who sell, and buy for yourselves" (Matthew 25:9 NKJV). But preparation cannot be made immediately. It takes time and will take the personal work of the Holy Spirit within. "But while they were going away to buy, the bridegroom came, and those who were prepared went in with him to the marriage feast; and the door was shut" (Matthew 25:10 AMP).

Those who were prepared went into the marriage feast with the bridegroom! One of the sobering thoughts of this parable is that all Christians are either wise or foolish. A Christian may think that he or she is a wise virgin, but the determining factor is not what one thinks. Rather, one should ask, "Has there been cooperation with the Lord in the time of preparation?" Remember, all ten were unmarried, virgin daughters. A person's Bible knowledge, how much he or she goes to church, how much the believer prays, or the individual's good works are not necessarily qualifying factors. Is there a heart of cooperation with the Lord in His personal dealing? Has the Lord been able to have His way in the heart, or is there a heart of rebellion like the Israelites who were in the wilderness?

The door "was shut" (*kleio*), which indicates that the door was shut and secured. The Septuagint, which is the Greek version of the Old Testament, uses this Greek word when Noah, his family, and all the animals went into the ark and the Lord "shut him in." The usage of this word in classical Greek carries the idea of safely securing whatever is shut up behind the doors. So too the Lord shut and secured the door so that even the pleading of the foolish virgins was not able to open it.

To qualify for the marriage, one must be prepared! Preparation does not occur through one method alone but through various means in which the Holy Spirit works in the willing heart to prepare the Christian for the marriage.

The Song of Songs

There are different ways to view the Song of Songs (Song of Solomon). For example, some view it only as the literal love between Solomon and the Shulamite. Some view it as the love of the Lord for Israel, and others see it as an allegory portraying the love relationship between the Lord and His betrothed, the bride of Christ. As are the facets of a diamond, it would seem that multiple views and different truths are possible from this book. It seems that there is more in this book than just a love relationship between Solomon and the Shulamite. For our purposes, we will view this as an allegory depicting Christ and His betrothed.

The Shulamite and the daughters of Jerusalem communicate and interact together, yet there are differences between them. Their relationship to the beloved is different. They have very different views of the beloved based on their proximity to him in relationship.

The Shulamite says, "I charge you, O daughters of Jerusalem, If you find my beloved, that you tell him I am lovesick" (Song of Solomon 5:8 NKJV).

The daughters of Jerusalem say, "What is your beloved more than another beloved, O fairest among women? What is your beloved more than another beloved, That you so charge us?" (Song of Solomon 5:9 NKJV).

There is quite a contrast between how the betrothed sees her beloved and how the daughters of Jerusalem see Him. The daughters of Jerusalem cannot understand what the betrothed sees in the beloved. It is hidden to them! In their current relationship they could not qualify for the marriage to Solomon. Their love for him is different.

Someone in close relationship with the Lord will see Him much differently than one who is not as close to Him. It is not that the Lord wants it that way. Rather it is a choice of the person to come near to Him.

In Song of Solomon, when the betrothed arrives at the wedding hall, she does not just walk in off the street, ready to be the bride. There is great significance in what precedes her entrance to the wedding hall and marriage.

The book begins in chapter 1, verse 2, with the Shulamite saying, "Let him kiss me with the kisses of his mouth." This shows that there has already been an ongoing relationship established between them. They have not just met. Below is a list of some of what qualifies her for the marriage:

1) (Song of Solomon 1:2) She shows the strong desire for him that is necessary for their relationship to develop further.
2) (Song of Solomon 1:4) "Draw me." In the heart, there is an attraction to her beloved that says, "I want to go further and deeper in this relationship."
3) (Song of Solomon 1:6) "But my own vineyard have I not kept." There was personal failure, but she rose above that to continue to walk with her beloved.

4) (Song of Solomon 1:7) She has a sincere heart to know him and to learn his ways.
5) (Song of Solomon 1:14) The betrothed has not just heard about him. She has experienced him.
6) (Song of Solomon 1:15–16) "Behold." The betrothed is beholding the bridegroom and sees his goodness (2 Corinthians 3:18).
7) (Song of Solomon 1:17) Quality material is used in the building process.
8) (Song of Solomon 2:3) The betrothed has learned to sit before him.
9) (Song of Solomon 2:4) She lives according to her beloved's banner or standard.
10) (Song of Solomon 2:10) There is obedience to his word.
11) (Song of Solomon 3:1–2) There is a seeking heart.
12) (Song of Solomon 3:4) After seeking her bridegroom and finding him, she will not let him go.

There seems to be more hidden in this book than the love between Solomon and the Shulamite. We may learn things about marriage, but there is more in the Song of Solomon than marriage principles for today. Something deeper is moving! The betrothed arrives at the marriage hall, prepared to become the bride. She has grown in her relationship with Solomon, and now is ready for the marriage.

As the Shulamite prepared her heart for Solomon so too is the church to prepare its heart. The Lord will use many different methods to produce the quality that He is looking for in His bride. He will use circumstances and His personal approach, to bring to us the opportunity to be prepared.

Greek Verbs

In the Greek, verbs in subjunctive mood suggest that the action is subject to some condition or makes an assertion about which there is some doubt, uncertainty, or indefiniteness. Simply defined, the subjunctive mood is the mood of possibility and potentiality. The action described may or may not occur, depending upon circumstances.

Subjunctive mood does apply many times in the New Testament. We can see this meaning in English through the following scriptures translated by the words *might, may,* and *should.* In the following scriptures the underlined words are subjunctive mood verbs:

> "For God sent not his Son into the world to condemn the world; but that the world through Him <u>might</u> be saved" (John 3:17 KJV). It is possible that those in the world would respond to the Son of God and be saved. Salvation is in the realm of possibility for everyone in the world, but they must receive Christ as Savior.

> "That the righteousness of the law <u>might</u> be fulfilled in us, who walk not after the flesh, but after the Spirit" (Romans 8:4 KJV). It is possible for the righteousness of the law to be fulfilled in us, but it is not a sure thing. The condition is walking according to the Spirit.

> "That being justified by his grace, we <u>should</u> be made heirs according to the hope of eternal life" (Titus 3:7 KJV). "We should be made" indicates that there are conditions to becoming an heir in reality. It is possible but not necessarily a sure thing.

> "But let patience have its perfect work, that you <u>may</u> be perfect and complete, lacking nothing" (James 1:4 NKJV). To be perfect (mature) will necessitate letting endurance have its full work.

> "That he <u>might</u> present it to himself a glorious church, not having spot, or wrinkle, or any such thing; but that

it should be holy and without blemish" (Ephesians 5:27 KJV). In Ephesians 5:27, the subjunctive mood verbs make an assertion about which there is some doubt. There is no doubt that the Lord will present to Himself a glorious church, but will He be able to bring every saved one into this arrangement? His wife should be holy and without blemish, but we know that there are Christians who do not live holy lives and have little interest in the things of God. Regardless of how much the Lord tries to work with them, they are not moldable, and they remain in their current shapes, not changing into the image of Jesus Christ, even though they are saved. The Lord will have a wife who is holy and without blemish, but not everyone who is saved will choose to walk with the Lord in holiness.

In the New Testament the subjunctive mood is often used. Many times it is used to show that the action is possible but not necessarily a sure thing. This mood suggests that for many scriptures there are certain qualifications to meet to bring about the desired end.

The active voice verb is also revealing in that the subject is the one performing the action. For example, you can consider the following passage: "Let us be glad and rejoice and give Him glory, for the marriage of the Lamb has come, and His wife has made herself ready" (Revelation 19:7 NKJV). The Greek verb translated "has made ready" is an active voice verb, which means that the bride must perform some actions to be ready. It is not just automatic. There must be cooperation with the Lord, and she must go through certain processes that change her heart, without which she would not be prepared. We are to do our part in the process to surrender with humble spirits and allow Jesus to make the needed changes within us through whatever methods He chooses. This verse is referring to Jesus' wife, those collectively who are ready for the union, those who have gone through whatever was necessary to personally be ready.

So both the subjunctive mood and the active voice verbs point toward the responsibility of the Christian to meet certain conditions or perform some action deemed necessary by the Lord.

In Jesus' ministry He did much teaching, and through His teaching He excluded many. This was not the purpose of the teaching. It was not what the Lord wanted, but through the rejection of His words, many excluded themselves. We can see one example in John 6. When Jesus was teaching, His words revealed the hearts of those who listened (John 6:26). The motive behind their seeking Jesus was not what it should have been. As He continued to teach, He said that He was the bread of life and that if they did not eat His flesh and drink His blood, there would be no life in them (John 6:53). The response to Jesus' teaching was that many of His disciples walked away from Him.

"From that time many of His disciples went back, and walked with Him no more" (John 6:66 NKJV). In the above scripture, the word *time* is not in the original Greek but was inserted by the translators. This could read, from that "saying" many of his disciples went back and no longer walked with Him.

What Jesus taught (His sayings) some disciples thought was too difficult for them to receive, so they rejected His Word. Those disciples who walked no more with Jesus disqualified themselves from all that they could have obtained by walking with the Lord. They pushed aside the time of their preparation because they did not agree with or receive the teaching of the Lord. To follow and to know the Lord will require a heart that continues even when there is lack of understanding. The apostles remained with the Lord because they knew He had the words of eternal life, even though they did not understand.

There are Christians today that fall into the same pattern that we see in John 6. They hear the Word and may even agree with it for a time; however, when something comes that they do not understand or agree with, they walk in another direction, and their hearts move toward the world and never respond favorably again. Because of the sayings of Christ, they walk no more with Jesus. This is a sad reality in many churches, and no matter how much you want to see a change of heart, too often it does not occur.

The Lord desires that every Christian walk with Him, no matter what comes his or her way, no matter what the Lord says, and no matter what the circumstance may be. Whether we understand His words, His will, or His way should have no relevance in serving or walking with Him. To be prepared for the union with Christ, it is necessary to walk faithfully with Him in the trials, in persecution, in the valley, as well as in the good, on the mountain, and in the blessings. We need to keep our hearts always toward Him in every situation of life. The heart that has Jesus as the main focus will go through the ordained arrangements of God and be, knowingly or unknowingly, prepared for the marriage with Christ, for they will have undergone the very things that will qualify them for the marriage.

CHAPTER 8

WITHOUT SPOT

Leprosy is a contagious, extremely ugly, and terrifying disease. It affects the nerves and causes inflammation under the skin, while white patches (lesions) appear on the skin. There is also a wasting away of body parts. In the Old Testament the one who was suspected of having leprosy was brought to the priest, who would determine whether the individual did or did not have it. If the sore did not appear to be more than skin deep, the priest would put him in isolation for seven days. On the seventh day the priest examined him again and isolated him another seven days. Then after those seven days if the sore was fading and not spreading, the priest would pronounce him clean. If the sore had spread, the priest pronounced him unclean—having an infectious disease. The priest was to look to see if there was a scab, and if so, he was to pronounce that it was leprosy.

We can make a spiritual comparison between leprosy and sin. Just because one had leprosy did not mean that he or she had sinned (Job 2:7-8, Luke 13:1–5, and John 9:1–7). The Lord chose leprosy to represent sin in all its ugliness as well as in its pollution and contamination. Leprosy is like sin in that it begins in a small way, progresses in degrees, and results in death. With leprosy there is a slow consumption of the body. The skin has lesions. Body parts begin to decay. The nose sinks. Gums rot. Teeth disappear. Hands and feet whither, and hair falls out. It is the same with sin. One's whole nature begins to rot and wastes away.

God used the ugliness of leprosy to portray the fact that sin can become exceedingly sinful. Sin is very ugly to God! Spiritually speaking,

God views the sinner as unclean, but many times Christians do not view their sin as such. It is said that leprosy does not produce pain like other diseases. If so, that also relates to sin in that sin can go on for a long time without inflicting any discernable pain. Sin can be contagious and it can possibly spread through contact.

Other people in the church can become vulnerable to the infection. If this infection were in the church, the pastor or leaders would have to take action for the good of the church. If there is a change (repentance), the individual can become clean or accepted. True repentance turns rejection into acceptance and cleanness.

The Lord Jesus is going to present to Himself a church with no spot or wrinkle. When one sees the church today, it may seem as though this is an impossible task. But we serve a wonderful Savior who has the ability to transform us into that which we cannot perceive or even believe possible. He has tools in His toolbox that He uses to do a particular job, and He has the skills to get the job done correctly.

In 2 Peter 2:13, Peter mentions those who were in the church and were eating with them in their fellowship meals. Those who Peter was referring to were walking according to the flesh. They were spots and blemishes, exhibiting sin in their conduct. Sin (Hebrews 10:26) in its leprous forms must be eliminated in order for there to be a church without spot.

In the classical Greek the word *spot* was used in the sense of impurity. Paul's usage of the word *spot* in Ephesians 5:27 relates to character blemishes that are not to be present in His called-out ones. Holiness is an essential characteristic of the Lord that must be in those who make up the church that Jesus presents to Himself—the one He holds in great honor. She has taken on the character of the Lord Himself and has become reflective of His glory, making her a glorious church.

There was an offering in Leviticus for the healed leper in order for him or her to become clean. There were two birds necessary for this offering. The priest killed one, and the other he freed so that he could pronounce the leper clean. One represented death. The other bird represented resurrection. The typology is not difficult to understand.

There must be a death to self to bring about a resurrection. Only as the Christian dies to self and functions in resurrection life can he or she hope to become spotless!

Our Obedience

In examining the offerings in the Old Testament, one of the necessary components for a blood sacrifice was that the animal had to be without spot or blemish (Numbers 19:2). To have an effective offering that is accepted, it had to comply with God's instructions. What the individual thought or the way that he or she felt the offering should be was not the bases of the offering. The priests offered it according to divine arrangement, according to the instructions given to Moses for each of the offerings.

There is an example in 1 Samuel where King Saul was told by the Lord, through the prophet Samuel, to heed the voice of the words of the Lord and utterly destroy the Amalekites and not spare anything alive. Instead, Saul spared their king and allowed the people to spare the best of all the animals. Samuel came to Saul and said,

> So Samuel said: Has the Lord as great delight in burnt offerings and sacrifices, as in obeying the voice of the Lord? Behold, to obey is better than sacrifice, and to heed than the fat of rams. For rebellion is as the sin of witchcraft, and stubbornness is as iniquity and idolatry. Because you have rejected the Word of the Lord, He also has rejected you from being king. (1 Samuel 15:22-23 NKJV)

This was not the first time that Saul had disobeyed. Samuel instructed Saul to wait for him to offer the burnt offering. Samuel was the one who functioned as a judge, prophet, and priest. In 1 Samuel 13, Saul and Israel were outnumbered and afraid of the mighty army of the

Philistines. Because Samuel delayed his coming, Saul, a Benjaminite, forced himself to serve in the capacity of priest, which God had entrusted only to the Levites. When Samuel arrived, his first words to Saul were these: "What have you done?" (1 Samuel 13:11 NKJV).

> And Samuel said to Saul, You have done foolishly. You have not kept the commandment of the Lord your God, which He commanded you. For now the Lord would have established your kingdom over Israel forever. But now your kingdom shall not continue. The Lord has sought for Himself a man after His own heart, and the Lord has commanded him to be commander over His people, because you have not kept what the Lord commanded you. (1 Samuel 13:13–14 NKJV)

God rejected Saul as king because he had a history of disobedience. The Lord tested Saul, and Saul failed. Without obedience to the Lord, the Christian will not go very far in God. Obeying the Lord is foundational to growth and is necessary in the process of purification to keep our garments spotless. "The Lord will establish you as a holy people to Himself, just as He has sworn to you, if you keep the commandments of the Lord your God and walk in His ways" (Deuteronomy 28:9 NKJV).

The whole premise for entering into the Promised Land was the obedience of the Israelites to the commandments of the Lord. The promises and blessings were sure and steadfast as long as the Israelites would do their part. Their part was to observe His commandments and statutes, to hear and do what the Lord said, and through their obedience, the Lord would establish them as a holy people unto Himself.

The Lord said that if they were disobedient, they would be "only oppressed" and "crushed continually." Moving in disobedience will cause the curses to pursue and overtake the individual. "But it shall come to pass, if you do not obey the voice of the Lord your God, to observe carefully all His commandments and His statutes which I command you today, that all these curses will come upon you and overtake you" (Deuteronomy 28:15 NKJV).

All disobedience has one thing in common. The individual puts the desires of the flesh above the will of God. This pattern began in the garden of Eden with Adam and Eve and continues to this day. All men have become sons of disobedience (Ephesians 2:2), and the stubborn heart of man will not acknowledge the authority and Lordship of Jesus Christ.

> But for those who are self-seeking and self-willed and disobedient to the truth but responsive to wickedness, there will be indignation and wrath. [And] there will be tribulation and anguish and calamity and constraint for every soul of man who [habitually] does evil, the Jew first and also the Greek (Gentile). But glory and honor and [heart] peace shall be awarded to everyone who [habitually] does good, the Jew first and also the Greek (Gentile). (Romans 2:8–10 AMP)

The Christian should not have a heart of disobedience. Instead, he or she should strongly desire to please the Lord and obey His commands, cooperating with Him. "How can a young man cleanse his way? By taking heed according to Your word" (Psalm 119:9 NKJV).

The guarantee that the Lord will accept the sacrifice of your life is your obedience. We are to present our lives unto God—holy, devoted, and well-pleasing to Him. As the Christian is obedient to the Word of the Lord, it has a cleansing effect and breaks the heart's desire to walk in a self-determined direction.

Disobedience (sin) leads to death, but obedience moves to righteousness. Jesus learned obedience through the things that He suffered, and we will learn obedience the same way. Some type of suffering will accompany obedience—if nothing more than suffering the loss of our own will in a circumstance. The individual Christian decides whether he will obey or disobey the Lord and walk in his or her direction and way. If we take heed to His Word, we will find the cleansing and purification that the seeking heart desires. It cannot be over emphasized how important our obedience is. It is a matter of spiritual life and death!

Be Ye Perfect

Is it possible for the Christian to be perfect? When we hear this question asked, the immediate response, of course, is that we cannot be perfect. A perfect Christian does not exist.

In Matthew 19:21 (NKJV), Jesus said to the rich young man, "If you want to be perfect, go, sell what you have and give to the poor, and you will have treasure in heaven; and come, follow Me."

If it were not possible for this man to be perfect, why would Jesus say that it was possible and direct him in that way? Jesus also taught at the Sermon on the Mount and said, "Be perfect, therefore, as your heavenly Father is perfect" (Matthew 5:48 NIV). Why would Jesus teach something that is a total impossibility?

The Old Testament was translated from Hebrew and the New Testament from the Greek. The translators tried to use the best English words to convey the meaning of the word in the original manuscripts. In every language over the course of time, certain words are no longer used. We can see this clearly by reading the King James Version of the Bible, which was translated from 1604 to 1611. Some of the Elizabethan English words are no longer in use today, and some of the words have different meanings than they did when it was written.

One of the problems that arises today is that we take an English word definition and apply it to the Bible. We take the meaning of the word in English and think that it is an exact match to the Greek word, and many times it is inaccurate and gives a meaning that was never intended from the original text. The word *perfect* is one example of this.

The English definition of the word perfect is as follows: "to be without faults or shortcomings." If we apply this definition to the Christian, then it is true that there is no such thing as a perfect Christian. But an examination of the Greek word translated by the English word *perfect* gives quite a different meaning.

Some of the meanings of the Greek word translated *perfect* are as follows: "grown up, mature, adult, not lacking any moral quality, complete in character." Now we can see that it is possible to be perfect in the biblical sense of the word. We are to grow, mature, and become spiritual adults. "For in many things we offend all. If any man offend not in word, the same is a perfect (or mature) man, and able also to bridle the whole body" (James 3:2 KJV). You can also consider the following: "Whom we preach, warning every man, and teaching every man in all wisdom; that we may present every man perfect in Christ Jesus" (Colossians 1:28 KJV). The hope of the apostle Paul was to present the church perfect (mature) to Christ. Through his personal suffering, teaching, and preaching Paul hoped to present every person in the church, full-grown to Christ.

Paul may or may not be able to bring these Christians to maturity. "But solid food is for the mature" (Hebrews 5:14 NIV).

"I press toward the mark for the prize of the high calling of God in Christ Jesus. Let us therefore, as many as be perfect (mature), be thus minded" (Philippians 3:14–15 KJV).

Every Christian should be moving toward perfection. Each should be developing in spirit and leaving childhood. But this does not always occur. Many hindrances plague this pilgrim walk. We must determine that we will walk with God, and by that I mean that we are to hear, follow, and obey the Lord in what we know and in what He personally shows us. Becoming perfect does not automatically take place. It will take diligence and steadfastness in the midst of all of life's circumstances, allowing the Holy Spirit to work for us, in us, and through us. Perfection—that is spiritual growth and character maturity—does not automatically take place after the judgment. Spiritual maturity and development in the character of Christ takes place here in this life, and what the Lord does within we carry throughout eternity.

"Jesus said to him, If you want to be perfect—" (Matthew 19:21 NKJV). "You want" is a present tense verb, not a future tense verb as follows: "If you want to be perfect in the future."

Refining

The very word *refine* tells us that some metal or liquid is not in its purest state and that some work will need done to change it. Purifying an impure material takes knowledge of the material and knowledge of the process needed to bring about the desired product. Our Lord looks at the heart, sees the impure state, and knows exactly what to do to change it from something undesirable to something precious. "He will sit as a refiner and a purifier of silver; He will purify the sons of Levi, and purge them as gold and silver, that they may offer to the Lord an offering in righteousness" (Malachi 3:3 NKJV).

The Hebrew word translated by the word *refiner* has various definitions, all of which have one thought in common, namely that there is some type of distress involved. In the refining process the pure metal needs to be separated from the impurities in the ore, and this is done in the smelting process. When the ore melts, and oxidizes, it forms a layer of impurities that float to the surface. Dross can contain a variety of unwanted impurities, some of which can be toxic.

The separation and discarding of the impurities can take place. In the Old Testament this procedure is mentioned as a symbol of God's purification process. In Jeremiah 9:7 and Zechariah 13:9, this process related to the nation of Israel when God sent hardship and affliction upon them in punishment for their sins.

In Job 23:10, refinement is to bring greater purification to the metal, referring to Job, and this can apply to the heart of the Christian. This work of separation is necessary in the church today because of the influence of the world upon the hearts of so many. This is not referring to some easy process that one does instantly, and then it is over. No, it will involve time and the fire of God placed upon the metal. The Refiner of metals is sitting at His fire, ready to work on the imperfections, and will increase the heat when He sees necessary in order to bring to the top that which pollutes.

How does this apply to us today? The Lord knows what work needs to be done. He sees the impurities of our hearts and will do whatever He needs to do. We do not need to pray for Him to remove from us the dross that hinders our relationship with Him. We may never pray that prayer because we do not want to experience suffering or adversity. But He is faithful and will act for us! "For You, O God, have tested us; You have refined us as silver is refined" (Psalm 66:10 NKJV).

We serve God, who is able to work in the lives of His people, and He can do what we are incapable of doing. We must not focus upon the process—the fire, the heat, the duration—but we are to keep our eyes upon our loving Father, who does all things well. To have pure gold and silver, a time of preparation is necessary. The removal of the dross will guarantee a better outcome, and the finished product will be that which is precious. The result of the refining process will be a heart purified for Him—a garment that has been cleansed and is spotless.

The Lord is not limited to fire as the only process to deal with impurity. There are many kingdom principles that the Christian is to walk in that will bring great benefit. One common theme that is necessary for purification is that the Christian's heart needs to be changed. As genuine change takes place, these principles will bring inner refinement of character that is necessary to prepare one for the marriage.

Or Any Such Thing

Jesus cares for you and desires that there is nothing between your heart and Him. He desires holiness in the church. Holiness is not just to be a word that we read in the Bible but is to be a key characteristic that is in the Christian. "Draw near to God and He will draw near to you.

Cleanse your hands, you sinners; and purify your hearts, you double-minded" (James 4:8 NKJV).

The words *cleanse* and *purify* appear in the Greek in the command form. How can we do these things, or does God do them for us and we play no part? Actually we do something, and so does the Lord. We surrender and desire for the Lord to cleanse and purify us. He sees the desire of the heart and works to accomplish it.

Have you ever wondered why the Lord gives so much attention to the little details of your life? If you have been a Christian for a while and really desire the Lord and your focus is on Him, you will find that He brings actions and attitudes under scrutiny and shows what is in your heart. "But we all, with unveiled face, beholding as in a mirror the glory of the Lord, are being transformed into the same image" (2 Corinthians 3:18 NKJV).

There is something special that takes place with those who behold the Lord. As we see the reflection of the Father in Jesus Christ, an unveiling of our heart occurs. This can be a very difficult experience, seeing the dross that is within come to the surface. Now what do we do? The Lord does this not to condemn but to show us our need for Him and to remove what we are powerless to remove ourselves. It is important to keep our eyes upon Jesus and not the dross because if we place our attention upon Him, He can accomplish the purification. This is a beautiful work of the Holy Spirit that we as Christians should covet. Christlike character is not automatic from just being a Christian. There are different processes that will take a multitude of circumstances, bringing opportunity our way that has the potential to produce character.

I was once in a situation at work in which I reacted in a way that many would say was justified, but the Lord thought differently. Before I walked ten feet away, the Lord touched my heart to turn and make the situation right. Christians would not consider what I did sin. Nor was it sin in the Lord's eyes. It came from a lack of character in my heart that the Lord wanted to change. "That He might present her to Himself a glorious church, not having spot or wrinkle or any such thing" (Ephesians 5:27 NKJV).

There is one phrase in this verse that is very revealing, and that is "or any such thing." We know that the glorious church that is presented to Christ is to be without spot or wrinkle, but why add this phrase? The "any such thing" would be anything that affects one's character. The Lord begins to deal with and change things not normally considered sin. This refers to the tweaking and fine-tuning the Lord must do to prepare His bride. There may be things that were okay when you were a younger Christian that now the Lord brings to the forefront in order to bring about a change that will bring greater conformity to the character of Christ. Others may not understand what the Lord is doing, but He is interested in every detail of our lives and will work to produce the highest quality that He can. In John 15, the pruning of the branch does not produce more fruit in quantity but more fruit of higher quality. Jesus is interested in quality fruit within the Christian, those who have gone through processes that have made them containers of His character (Romans 8:28–29).

Only the Lord Jesus can produce the fruit of quality of character. The Lord desires that His people have holy character that is Christlike. To that end Christians are to obey. Jesus will do His part to refine, tweak, and fine-tune hearts and to bring people to godly maturity.

He truly is wonderful and loving to us and will do exceeding abundantly above all that we can ask or think. Jesus hungers for great surrender from our hearts so that He can do in us what will bring intimacy with Him. The inner work of the Holy Spirit on yielded hearts will lead to the fellowship and intimacy desired by those who long for the Lord.

CHAPTER 9

FINE LINEN

Consider the following: "Can a virgin forget her ornaments, or a bride her attire?" (Jeremiah 2:32 KJV). "Can a maid forget and neglect [to wear] her ornaments, or a bride her [marriage] girdle [with its significance like that of a wedding ring]?" (Jeremiah 2:32 AMP).

In the natural world a bride does not forget to be properly dressed, but this can occur in spirit! Marriage is one of the most important relationships into which a person can enter, but in many instances there are inadequate preparations made before the marriage. In the natural world more preparation is made for the wedding ceremony and reception than the relationship itself. It comes as no surprise that so many marriages end in divorce. The time preceding marriage is extremely important because it is the time when the foundation for the marriage is built. However, what foundation can the Lord lay?

There can be different foundations built. At the Sermon on the Mount, Jesus sat down and began to teach His disciples. One of the topics He addressed was the foundation of one's life. He stressed the importance of building one's house on the proper support. Everyone's life has a foundation, but what type is it? Are you building your house upon the sand or upon the rock? No one would be so foolish to place a heavy structure on sand without some solid base upon which to rest. We understand that sand is shaky and shifting, and rock is steady and solid. In the natural, everyone understands the importance of a proper foundation to support a building, but common sense is lost when it comes to the spiritual realm.

If we take the same natural thinking related to a proper foundation and apply it to disobedience to the Lord, we could say that those who do not keep His sayings are foolish. Those who hear the sayings of Jesus and do not do them are like those who build their houses on the sand. They are doing that which will cause the collapse of their house. The rock represents those who hear the sayings of Jesus and do them. We build a good foundation through properly hearing and doing what the Lord says. When the foundation is correct in one's life, the Lord can begin to build in other areas, such as marriage. Today many build their marriages upon the sinking sand of self-centeredness. Both spouses are in the marriage for what they can get out of it. Many believe that marriage is a fifty-fifty proposition. This leaves room for self-centeredness to flourish, and to be present at least 50 percent of the time. Rather it should be 100 percent, where the husband and wife give all for each other. For marriage to be successful in the eyes of the Lord, building on the foundation of Jesus Christ is fundamental and not upon any other person or thing. If this principle of giving 100 percent is not functioning in our hearts and in our marriages, how can it function correctly when it comes to our relationship with the Lord and our marriage to Him?

In Revelation 18, before the introduction of the Lamb's wife, there is the judgment of the great harlot Babylon. The great whore, who is a type of the world system, epitomizes the great moral ruin and destruction seen in the earth. She is seen clothed in the fine linen of the world, and she has given that linen to those who have emulated her. Her worldly influence has reached to the very core of those who have placed their gaze upon her, and the closeness of relationship with her has become the source of the merchants weeping when they see her destroyed (Revelation 18:11). One of the core characteristics found in the great harlot and in the worldly heart of man is self-centeredness.

In contrast to the great harlot, there is the bride, the Lamb's wife. In the bride is seen the embodiment of the essential characteristics of Jesus, which makes her cherished by the Lord. There can be no counterfeit. No substitute will suffice. She has been clothed with inner quality, and she gives her all for Jesus. She has gone through the making process and has undergone the needed changes to make her ready for the marriage. "Let us be glad and rejoice and give Him glory, for the marriage of the Lamb has come, and His wife has made herself ready" (Revelation 19:7 NKJV).

Note that the glory goes to Jesus for His wife's readiness. She has done her part in surrender, in cooperation, and in being under God's dealings, having walked with Him in the difficult places. He does His part in making her what she could not be apart from Him. He receives the glory for her becoming glorious!

Under His watchful eye, she has made herself ready, and because she is ready, certain things are given to her. "And to her it was granted to be arrayed in fine linen, clean and bright, for the fine linen is the righteous acts of the saints" (Revelation 19:8 NKJV).

She receives fine, bright white linen because she has qualified for this privilege. She is properly dressed because she did what was necessary to become ready and prepared. Readiness precedes the giving of the fine linen!

The fine linen represents the righteous acts of the saints. *Louw & Nida Greek-English Lexicon* defines a righteous act as an act that is in accordance with what God requires. A righteous act would be one that is done through the leading of the Spirit and not initiated by the individual (Matthew 7:22). The leading of the Spirit will inevitably bring us through times of testing by fire, times that are essential in the refining process, and this will provide riches and white garments for us. "I counsel you to buy from Me gold refined in the fire, that you may be rich; and white garments, that you may be clothed, that the shame of your nakedness may not be revealed" (Revelation 3:18 NKJV).

Jesus addresses the church of the Laodiceans and gives them instruction to acquire white garments. The first thing He says is, "Buy of Me." This will necessitate Jesus as the main focus of the heart, for He is the only One that can provide what is needed to clothe the Christian. Purchasing gold refined in the fire is next. "Buy the truth, and sell it not" (Proverbs 23:23 KJV). Gold is purchased in the fire of circumstances, and in the Bible the testing of one's faith is said to be extremely valuable, more than the value of gold (1 Peter 1:7). Testing by fire has the potential to purify the heart in such a way that the works that are done become the righteous acts of the saints. These works are considered by the Lord as good works because the heart has been purified by fire (Ephesians 2:10; Titus 2:14, 3:8).

In Isaiah 55, it says to come and buy without money and without price. We cannot purchase spiritual things with the money of this world. We can spend the money of this world on that which is not really the bread that we need because physical bread (things) cannot satisfy the inner need of the soul. The purchase of spiritual wine and milk are without money. There is another means by which we can purchase them.

Attaining white garments will come with a price that is paid in the refining fire of God. We must faithfully walk with God in His will for our lives to be able to purchase them. The cost is that which is most precious to us—our life, our will, our focus, our time, our choices, our desires, etc. "And I will bring the third part through the fire, and will refine them as silver is refined, and will try them as gold is tried: they shall call on My name, and I will hear them: I will say, it is My people: and they shall say, the Lord is my God" (Zechariah 13:9 KJV). You can also consider the following: "Behold, I have refined you, but not as silver; I have tested you in the furnace of affliction" (Isaiah 48:10 NKJV).

In Isaiah 48:10, the furnace of affliction to Israel was what they experienced in Babylon. Our furnace of trouble would be in our circumstances where the Lord deals with each of us in a very specific way. He examines attitudes and motives in order to purify our hearts. That process of refining is an ongoing work of the Holy Spirit, which lays a foundation necessary to prepare Christians for the marriage.

In Revelation 19:8, the writer describes the refining process using different terminology, but it yields the same results. The meaning of the root word translated "fine linen" means "to bleach white". "Clean and bright" refers to the result of cleansing, purification, and washing that the bride has undergone. Because of the preparation of the heart, the bride receives fine linen. It is given to her not just because she has arrived at the marriage but rather because she has arrived in a certain condition that qualifies her to be given fine linen.

In Song of Solomon, the bride looks at the bridegroom and sees him as the finest gold (Song of Solomon 5:11, 14–15). That was a source of inspiration and influenced her to more fully surrender and become more like him. In the next chapter the bridegroom praises the beauty of the bride because of the work that has been accomplished within her (Song of Solomon 6:4–10). A change has taken place and her inner beauty is something to be treasured. She has become glorious.

Overcoming

As Jesus speaks to the seven churches in the book of Revelation, one of the things that He says to each of them is that they needed to overcome. Specifically in Revelation 3:5, He says that the person who overcomes shall be clothed in white garments. Overcoming is another qualifying factor in order to be clothed in white raiment. He does not say specifically what to overcome because there is not just one thing to overcome. It will vary from person to person and from circumstance to circumstance. But the one who is presently and continually overcoming in his or her circumstances will be clothed. Overcoming must always be done with the right attitude toward the Lord, people, and circumstances. We can have total victory over our enemies by loving them with the right attitudes and having the right hearts toward them. That is not to say that there can never be failure, but as the heart beholds Jesus and desires to be like Him, He can help us to overcome so that we can be properly clothed.

The way the Lord works within is truly marvelous, but the Christian is always in present danger by the flesh spotting his or her garments. All of the wonderful work the Lord does and all the great changes that are done within can be reversed by the flesh. It is very sad to see a Christian who has walked with God for some time turn aside and move in the flesh, believing that everything is fine, only to allow the flesh to spot his or her garment. It does not have to be so. We can walk with Jesus and stay in the will of God and overcome the world, the flesh, and the

Devil. "But He knows the way that I take; When He has tested me, I shall come forth as gold" (Job 23:10 NKJV).

Testing of the heart is not a bad thing. At times Christians think that they have done something wrong when they are tested. No, testing is necessary for different reasons, one being so that people may see their hearts and allow the Lord to change them.

Paul had the burden of the churches upon his heart. He labored endlessly to bring them further in the faith and to see them develop spiritually. Paul had a godly zeal that caused him to give his all to the Lord and to the churches. "For I am jealous for you with godly jealousy. For I have betrothed you to one husband, that I may present you as a chaste virgin to Christ" (2 Corinthians 11:2 NKJV).

For the benefit of the church in spirit, Paul promised them in marriage to Christ. As an apostle of Jesus Christ, he did everything in his power to bring the churches to where this could become a reality. Paul desired to present the churches to Christ as a pure, chaste virgin. This would not occur automatically but would take cooperation and preparation on their behalf. "But I fear, lest somehow, as the serpent deceived Eve by his craftiness, so your minds may be corrupted from the simplicity that is in Christ" (2 Corinthians 11:3 NKJV). (*Simplicity* here means singleness or sincerity.)

The serpent works to corrupt the minds of Christians. He can corrupt the mind and easily influence one to move in a direction that is not of the Lord's choosing. The unsuspecting Christian can shift from the singleness of the gospel and begin to walk down a path toward compromise and worldly thinking. "I am afraid for you, lest I have labored for you in vain. (12) Brethren, I urge you to become like me" (Galatians 4:11-12 NKJV).

There seems to be many Christians today who are not prepared or have not received any teaching that they need to be prepared. They live their lives as though everything will automatically come to them and everything is theirs just because they are Christians. The thinking is that they will go to heaven, have everything, live happily ever after, and never suffer any loss. There may be quite a shock for some Christians who live their lives the way they want. There will be weeping because they will see what the Lord has offered, what was available to them, and what they missed. Because they walked their own ways, they never acquired certain characteristics of the Lord to qualify them for certain rewards or positions.

Paul said to the Philippians that he suffered the loss of all things in order to win Christ (Philippians 3:8). He said that he was pressing toward the mark for the prize of the high calling of God in Christ, and those who are mature should have the same mind as him and press toward the high calling. Then he says something that we should consider. "Brethren, be followers together of me, and mark them which walk so as ye have us for an ensample. (For many walk, of whom I have told you often, and now tell you even weeping, that they are the enemies of the cross of Christ)" (Philippians 3:17–18 KJV).

In contrast to verse 15, where Paul speaks of those who were mature, verse 18 refers to those who were not mature and walked contrary to the ways of the Lord. Paul does not say that these individuals were enemies of the Lord, the blessings, the good news, the church, or salvation. They were enemies of the cross! Not all Christians will deny themselves, pick up their cross daily, and follow the Lord (Luke 9:23). The cross was an instrument of death, and even today it is still repulsive because it demands one's life. Some are not willing to go that far. We see the same thought in Matthew 10, where Jesus is speaking to His disciples and says that one can follow Him and not take up his or her cross (Matthew 10:38).

"Whose end is destruction" (Philippians 3:19 NKJV). Paul was not saying that they were going to hell. The word *destruction* means spiritual loss. Those who want nothing to do with and avoid at all cost the processes and dealings of the Lord will suffer the loss of what those processes could have produced in their lives. Being an enemy of the cross (the death that must occur in one's life) will ultimately bring loss that the individual may regret later. "For whoever desires to save his life will lose it, but whoever loses his life for My sake will save it" (Luke 9:24 KJV).

Christians can abandon the true gospel, which tells us that we must lose our lives in this world. "I am crucified with Christ: nevertheless I live; yet not I, but Christ liveth in me: and the life which I now live in the flesh I live by the faith of the Son of God" (Galatians 2:20 KJV). We are to live our lives here, realizing that this life is not *for* this life. The Christian is to look away from the vanity of the world to the great value of the gospel, which can bring great richness now and for all eternity. Jesus is trying to prepare His bride today for eternity.

What was the purpose of the message of John the Baptist? He was the voice of one crying in the wilderness, "Prepare the way of the Lord; Make His paths straight" (Matthew 3:3 NKJV). He was not meaning to prepare some physical road but the road into the hearts of the people to receive the Lord. But what was John really trying to prepare by his life and message? "He will also go before Him in the spirit and power of Elijah, 'to turn the hearts of the fathers to the children,' and the disobedient to the wisdom of the just, to make ready a people prepared for the Lord" (Luke 1:17 NKJV).

He was preparing a people! Turning the hearts of the fathers to their children speaks of an inner change of the heart. It has been the same in every generation where the Lord has been at work preparing the hearts of believers, trying to prepare the way and a path into their hearts so that He can bring the changes that are necessary to dress them in fine linen.

Paul says to the Colossians to put off anger, wrath, malice, filthy language, etc., to put off the old man with all his evil deeds. Next he tells them to put on the new man who is renewed in knowledge after Christ (Colossians 3:8–10, 12). To the Ephesians he says to put off their previous manner of living and to put on the new nature that is created in God's image, in true righteousness and holiness (Ephesians 4:22, 24). The phraseology used by Paul typifies the removal of one garment and then to dress in another. The verb used in Colossians 3:8 "put off" is in the command form, which says to us that we have some responsibility in this matter. This is not automatic but requires some action on the part of the Christian, sometimes just his or her willingness in certain situations.

There is a secret place in Him that is unknown by many, a place where intimacy is hidden. Things occur there cannot be seen by the world, by the carnal Christian, and the uninterested Christians. Dwelling in the secret place of the most high is a place where we put off one garment and put on another! This is a place where the Lord has made all the provisions necessary for changing garments. In Song of Solomon, we read of such a place called the secret place of the stairs. "O my dove, that art in the clefts of the rock, in the secret places of the stairs, let me see thy countenance, let me hear thy voice; for sweet is thy voice, and thy countenance is comely" (Song of Solomon 2:14 KJV).

The Shulamite sees her lover in the clefts of the rock. These concealed strongholds are attainable only by change. The Beloved must make her feet like the feet of a deer so that she can walk on her high places to meet Him. These rocky, steep, secluded areas are spiritual places of intimacy and development, where deep relationship blossoms. These places are inaccessible through self-strength, self-determination, self-centeredness, or self-will, but they are reachable through surrender. The Lord brings one there! "He will make me to walk upon mine high places" (Habakkuk 3:19 KJV).

With Jesus these secret places can be found, and His ways will lead us to the steep, unreachable places where the Christian can begin to ascend. In Revelation 22, the Spirit and the bride say, "Come!" This call goes out to those who have responded to the salvation of the Lord and desire to draw closer to Jesus. The answer to this call is through preparation. The "I Am" of Revelation 22:16 is the One we must see and move toward with our hearts in order to bring the fulfillment of the preparation of the bride. "I am the Root and the Offspring of David, the Bright and Morning Star" (Revelation 22:16 NKJV).

Jesus is ever waiting for the church to awake! "Therefore He says: Awake, you who sleep, arise from the dead, and Christ will give you light" (Ephesians 5:14 NKJV). Finally you can also consider the following: "And do this, knowing the time, that now it is high time to awake out of sleep; for now our salvation is nearer than when we first believed" (Romans 13:11 NKJV).

CHAPTER 10

THE MARRIAGE

If we were to survey a number of Christians and ask the question, "What do you think people want the most in marriage?" we would probably get many different answers. But there are some answers that are common to most people.

True love: What is true love? One of the characteristics of love is that it is directional. It is to flow out from you toward your spouse, not looking for anything in return. This type of love becomes essential in laying the correct foundation to build a successful marriage. If love is operating in this manner, it becomes the basis for reciprocity. A marriage cannot survive and flourish without reciprocal love. "For God so loved the world that He gave His only begotten son" (John 3:16 NKJV). That directional love flowed from the Father through Christ to us, and became the foundation for our relationship with Him and makes possible the reciprocal love that we now enjoy.

Intimacy: In marriage, intimacy is not just sex. Intimacy is the connection we make in spirit through the will of God and the choice to be close. It moves deeply to where a couple knows that they are to be together, and they work to practice what strengthens their relationship.

Some Christians are not interested in intimacy with Christ, and their lives testify to that fact. So what makes them think that they will have an interest later in heaven? We are to grow in closeness with Christ in this life, and that intimacy will result in our union with Him.

Faithfulness: This same characteristic is to reside in the heart of the Christian. It is a fruit of the Spirit, and in Psalms it says, "For the Lord preserves the faithful" (Psalm 31:23 NKJV). Being faithful to one another in marriage becomes a pillar that will support the marriage. In an age when oftentimes this is missing, our faithfulness will testify to the faithfulness of the Lord, which He has placed within us. This characteristic is seen in the Father as related to man. He is loyal and dependable, bringing stability into the relationship. In the Bible it refers to Jesus as the faithful witness, faithful one, and the faithful high priest. He abides faithful!

Friendship: Friendship is a very important part of a relationship. A friend is more than a person you know well. He or she is someone whom you value and who values you. It is nice to know that out there is someone that you can count on when you cannot count on anyone else. A person who has friends must show him or herself friendly. There is one who sticks closer than anyone does, and His name is Jesus. No one will ever be a friend like Him, who will be there for you, remain loyal to death, and never let you down. However, for Him to be your friend, you must befriend Him and take the time to know Him. This friendship takes time, but it will be worth having Jesus as your friend.

Communication: If communication is missing in a relationship, it can cause enormous difficulty. Through proper interaction we can avoid many misunderstandings. For many communication must be practiced so that certain stumbling blocks do not cause a breakdown in relationship. Communication is very important and can really enhance marriage. Because we are acquainted with Jesus, there is an interaction with Him that reveals His will and ways and more importantly, Himself. The Lord will communicate to Christians in a way that they will understand to direct them in the way that they should go.

True love, intimacy, friendship, faithfulness, and communication are just some of the things that are to be present in a good marriage. These are just some of the things that should be active and growing in our relationship with Jesus and that will pave the way to our marriage with Him. These qualities will make for a healthy and happy marriage that will last for all eternity.

In the book of Ruth, Boaz the Bethlehemite was a man of wealth, generosity, kindness, virtue, and chastity. I believe he was patiently waiting for the Lord to prepare and send a wife to him, and at the appointed time the Lord brought Ruth into his fields. Prior to this, Ruth was a Moabite woman and a stranger to God from an idol-worshipping nation. She was busy with life's responsibilities when she encountered a needy circumstance with her mother-in-law, Naomi, and they both left Moab to go to Bethlehem. Through their time together, Ruth placed her trust in the God of Naomi and made Him her God. Before the Lord presented Ruth in marriage to Boaz, He worked in her life.

Here are some of the things that Ruth experienced that helped prepare her for her marriage with Boaz:

1) She had lost her husband (Ruth 1:4–5).

2) She had to decide whether to stay in her own country, Moab, or go with Naomi to a foreign land (Ruth 1:7).

3) She had to decide to leave her sister-in-law and probably her family (Ruth 1:9–13).

4) It appeared to her that following the Lord may cost her what she desired, which was the security of being married (Ruth1:16–17).

5) When she went with Naomi to Bethlehem, she willingly put herself in harm's way to do what was right to provide for her and Naomi (Ruth 2:2, 9, 22).

6) She found grace in the eyes of the Lord and in the eyes of Boaz (Ruth 2:10).

7) Her faith in God was tested (Ruth 2:11).

8) Her obedience and submission to Naomi was also tested (Ruth 3:4).

9) She experienced the possibility of humiliating rejection (Ruth 3:4).

10) She also experienced the possibility of her actions being misunderstood (Ruth 3:14).

11) She overcame the temptation to follow younger men (Ruth 3:10).

12) She also overcame the temptation to take matters into her own hands and do what she wanted.

The Lord had been working in her life to draw her close and, through these circumstances, to do in her what could not be possible otherwise. Ruth's correct response to the Lord in these circumstances was key to prepare her for marriage. Her decision to walk with God regardless of personal sacrifice became the foundation the Lord could build upon. Her personal acknowledgment of God, commitment to do what was right concerning Naomi, decision to ignore her desire to remarry and to go with Naomi back to Bethlehem showed the godly characteristic of selfless dedication. When we see her lying at the feet of Boaz, we know there is more to this than a story of love between two people.

We can draw an analogy between Boaz, who is a picture of the Lord Jesus in the Old Testament, and Ruth, who is a type of the bride of Christ. The Lord did much work in Ruth, and He does much work in the bride of Christ preparing her for her Husband. Her response to the leading of God makes Ruth ready, which demonstrates that the bride of Christ is to respond to Jesus so that she is also ready.

There is a similar story in the Song of Solomon when the Shulamite arrives in Solomon's presence after she has undergone many tests of her love for him. Without tests and trials, there could be some doubt as to the genuineness of love. The Shulamite has the assurance that her love for Solomon has stood the test and has even grown through the experience. Comparably the preparation of the bride of Christ is necessary, and she must go through whatever tests, tribulations, troubles, or temptations the Lord deems necessary to make her ready for the marriage. Through her cooperation, the bride of Christ will take on the likeness of Jesus, and that will be what makes her so attractive and gives her an indescribable beauty. "And the Spirit and the bride say, 'Come!' And let him who hears say, 'Come!' And let him who thirsts come" (Revelation 22:17 NKJV).

This is an offer to respond to the gospel of salvation. Moreover, it is a compelling cry to the heart of whoever will respond to be included in the special marriage to Jesus Christ. The answer to this call *come* is through the preparation of the individual Christian, and its fulfillment is in the union with Christ.

"Who are kept by the power of God through faith unto salvation ready to be revealed in the last time" (1 Peter 1:5 KJV). In this verse *who* is masculine plural. In pluralized situations the masculine is used for groups composed of both males and females. The *who* are the elect of God (v2) who are being kept in the power of God through faith unto salvation (the preparing process). When you come to the word *ready*, it is feminine singular, referring to the prepared one, the bride.

Ephesians 5:26–27 NKJV says, "That He might sanctify and cleanse her with the washing of water by the word that He might present her to Himself a glorious church, not having spot or wrinkle or any such thing, but that she should be holy and without blemish."

In verse 26, the word translated as *her* speaks of those who would become clean, washed, and be the bride. In verse 27, when Christ presents her to Himself, she will show forth His glory (as said in Psalm 45:13, which says, "The king's daughter is all glorious within") and becomes totally lost in Him. She must decrease. He must increase, and He becomes all!

In reading the book of Revelation, sometimes problems arise in understanding what John is meaning. We see symbolic language used to portray some truth. For example, Jesus is the Lamb of God. He is not literally a lamb, but the words are descriptive of the sacrifice of Jesus. Other examples are the seven lamp stands, which are the seven churches that are to carry the light to the world, and the seven stars, which are the messengers or pastors of the churches. Throughout the book of Revelation is similar symbolism.

In Revelation 21, what is "the New Jerusalem?" Some believe it is a physical structure created by God that will descend from heaven to earth. Others believe it is the future home of the Christian or that it is a new and greater Jerusalem to replace the old Jerusalem.

When John sees the New Jerusalem, he sees something never before seen, and he is trying to describe with words what he sees. Remember that he is seeing something in spirit that he is going to try to describe with language, which is a very difficult thing to do. If you have ever personally seen the glory of God, you will find that it is impossible to describe accurately what you have seen. You can try to describe it, but you will find that your words are insufficient. "And I, John, saw the holy city, New Jerusalem, coming down out of heaven from God, prepared as a bride adorned for her husband" (Revelation 21:2 NKJV). John describes a holy city that he calls the New Jerusalem. He likens it to a bride adorned for her husband. This word *adorned* means "to be beautiful by decorating (Louw, 1996), to be put in proper order (Vine, 1984)." *Thayer's Lexicon* defines this word as thus: "to make ready, to prepare."

The phraseology used hints of something other than a physical structure. It suggests that there is something much more than a physical city. "Then one of the seven angels who had the seven bowls filled with the seven last plagues came to me and talked with me, saying, "Come, I will show you the bride, the Lamb's wife" (Revelation 21:9 NKJV).

One of the angels says to John, "I will show you the bride." He does not say that he was going to show him some physical city or buildings. The angel shows him the bride. The Greek word *numphe* translated as *bride* means "one veiled as a bride is veiled" (Strong's, 1995). Many cannot see beyond this veil to recognize and understand who this is referring to.

"And he carried me away in the Spirit to a great and high mountain, and showed me the great city, the holy Jerusalem, descending out of heaven from God" (Revelation 21:10 NKJV). John was in spirit carried away. The angel says that he is going to show John the bride, the Lamb's wife, and he showed him "the great city, the holy Jerusalem, descending out of heaven." This city is not a city to live in but is representative of the bride of Christ in all her beauty, the one in whom Christ lives, composed of Christians who have become the bride.

"In whom you also are being built together for a dwelling place of God in the Spirit" (Ephesians 2:22 NKJV). Christians are being built together to become a dwelling place of God (1 Corinthians 3:9, 16). The bride, the Lamb's wife, whom the angel shows John, is that great city, the New Jerusalem!

"Having the glory of God—" (Revelation 21:11 NKJV). *Having* can reference holding and possessing the glory of God. This is expressive of what the bride has and testifies to the work of the Spirit that brought her into possession of His glory.

In the following scriptures, notice where Paul says the glory of God resides:

> "For our light affliction, which is but for a moment, is working for us a far more exceeding and eternal weight of glory" (2 Corinthians 4:17 NKJV). The apostle Paul calls the troubles of this life "our light affliction." These afflictions work a weight of glory into the Christian that they will possess for all eternity.

"To them God willed to make known what are the riches of the glory of this mystery among the Gentiles: which is Christ in you, the hope of glory" (Colossians 1:27 NKJV).

"And that He might make known the riches of His glory on the vessels of mercy, which He had prepared beforehand for glory" (Romans 9:23 NKJV).

"For I consider that the sufferings of this present time are not worthy to be compared with the glory which shall be revealed in us" (Romans 8:18 NKJV). (See also John 17:10.) In the previous scriptures, Paul is very emphatic as to where the glory of God resides. He says multiple times that the glory of God will be in you and does not mention any physical structure containing the glory of God.

"Behold, the tabernacle of God is with men" (Revelation 21:3 NKJV).

"When He comes to be glorified in His saints [on that day He will be made more glorious in His consecrated people], and [He will] be marveled at and admired [in His glory reflected] in all who have believed [who have adhered to, trusted in, and relied on Him]" (2 Thessalonians 1:10 AMP). The tabernacle of God is not some physical city. It is man who has become His habitation!

As we continue to read Revelation 21, difficulties arise for many Christians because of their thinking or the teaching they have had concerning the New Jerusalem. If one holds to the idea that the pattern of this city is after the model of some earthly city, then the gold, silver, and precious stone will fall right in line with their thinking of a physical structure.

If one believes that the angel is showing John the bride, the Lamb's wife, then the description of her magnificent beauty takes on a different light. In various places the Bible speaks of the testing of metal (gold and silver) to bring about purity. We have no problem believing and associating testing with trials that produce purity within the Christian. But when it comes to the New Jerusalem possessing the glory of God, we revert back to thinking of a physical structure. To have pure gold, it must be purified by fire, and the result of this testing is what is seen in Revelation 21:18–20.

"Having the glory of God: and her light was like (or similar in appearance or character) unto a stone most precious, even like a jasper stone, clear as crystal" (Revelation 21:11 KJV). Her light—the light of the glory of God—which the bride was given, has a beauty like precious stones. John is having great difficulty describing what he is seeing because of her tremendous beauty and because of her Christlike character. John begins to compare her to the most beautiful gems known to man. Consider the following passages:

> "You also, as living stones, are being built up a spiritual house" (1 Peter 2:5 NKJV). The building program is not a physical building but a living building—a spiritual house. That is not to say that there will not be a New Jerusalem that is a literal city, but the "New Jerusalem in Revelation 21 is something different.

> "For we are God's fellow workers; you are God's field, you are Gods building" (1 Corinthians 3:9 NKJV).

> "The city had no need of the sun or of the moon to shine in it, for the glory of God illuminated it. The Lamb is its light" (Revelation 21:23 NKJV). The word translated as *it* is a personal pronoun in the Greek and could be

translated as *her*. The glory of God is the main source of light that will emanate in and through her, the bride.

"Its gates shall not be shut at all by day" (Revelation 21:25 NKJV).

There is also a verse in Proverbs 23 that says, "As a man thinks in his heart, so is he." The word *thinks* means that the individual is to be like a gatekeeper who opens the gate to that which is good and beneficial and closes the gate to that which is harmful and would defile. The Christian is to act like the gatekeeper of his or her heart, opening and closing to what he should. The gates (hearts) of the city (those who make up the bride) will not have to shut anymore because of the removal of what can defile and the danger from contamination is past.

Revelation 21 seems to be speaking of the bride of Christ, the prepared one, the one upon whom the Lord has been working, and the one who has responded favorably to Him. If this is a picture of the bride, we as Christians want to do whatever we can to enhance our relationship with the Lord. We should desire to be prepared so that there will be no surprises such as the Lord locking the door (Matthew 25:10).

There will be those who are invited guests at the wedding but are not a part of the marriage. In Revelation 22:17, one of the meanings of the word *come* is to come into a particular state or condition, implying a process. There are those who have little interest in the processes the Lord uses to prepare people for the marriage. "For many are called, but few are chosen" (few become choice) (Matthew 22:14 NKJV).

We should have a desire to be married to the Lord and to go through whatever is necessary to transform our hearts into spiritual states that are presentable to Jesus Christ.

After the bride is ready, the marriage occurs! So we all should want to be included in the marriage and draw ever nearer in relationship with Jesus. The loud cry of the Spirit and the bride say, "Come!" Let us hear this cry today, respond to our Lord by giving Him what He requires, and follow on to know Him more. In our walk with the Lord, whatever we must endure or experience in this life can work for our good if we yield to Jesus and allow the Holy Spirit to work in our hearts. May Jesus create in us an overwhelming thirst that can only be quenched by His person (Revelation 21:6). The marriage will be so good, so right, and so wonderful. It will be beyond what we could ever imagine, and it will be worth whatever it may cost us in this life. Our response, dedication, sacrifice, and time will be well worth it, and the return on our investment will be far above what we could have conceived. May we continue to walk with the Lord in the easy and hard places, realizing that Jesus does all things well, knowing that He has our best interest in mind. We can have assurance that He will work in our lives to prepare us for the wondrous union with Him.

CONCLUSION

In *Preparing the bride of* Christ we have looked at God's personal call, our response, progression in the kingdom of God, and some of the processes for becoming. In addition, we looked at different hindering factors to our walk with God. To walk with God in the way He desires will entail our learning the ways of God. God made known His acts (miracles) to the children of Israel but to Moses He made known His ways. We should pray and ask God to show us His ways, and we will find that He will begin to reveal them to us in our circumstances. If we begin to see the ways of the Lord, it will be to our advantage because we will have the opportunity to cooperate with Him to a greater degree. The various topics we covered are important to see so that Christians can direct their steps in God's way.

Some Christians are more dedicated to what they want to do than to Jesus. If our preparation for the marriage is to occur, we must be dedicated to the Lord. Our devotion to Jesus and His kingdom will be crucial to meet certain conditions that will help prepare us as the bride. A new beginning with the Lord can take place no matter where we spiritually find ourselves today. "But exhort one another daily, while it is called "Today," lest any of you be hardened through the deceitfulness of sin (Hebrews 3:13 NKJV). "Thus says the Lord: In an acceptable time I have heard You, And in the day of salvation I have helped You" (Isa 49:8 NKJV). The Lord is always ready to receive the repentant heart and to draw close those who are willing. May we reach out to Him with sincere hearts and willing minds. Jesus is there to meet those who seek Him and create within them quality that was not there before. The Lord has provided everything necessary to prepare Christians for the marriage!

For example, kingdom principles that we find in the New Testament contain certain arrangements that if kept, will be instrumental in preparing the Christian.

It is the hope and prayer of this author that this book has directed the hearts of the readers to the Lord and caused Christians to look to the Lord with a heart that desires to be prepared for the marriage. We should not focus upon any of our shortcomings or past failures but upon Jesus Christ, who is the only one who can prepare His bride. All callings and all of the purposes of the Lord for our lives flow together toward and into the marriage to Christ. If we are ready, it will be a glorious day like we have never experienced, being brought into the unimaginable – our marriage to Jesus Christ. The Lord will have gathered a people prepared for the Lord. May we be attentive to the Lord Jesus Christ, permit Him to deal with us as only He can, and allow Him to prepare our hearts for this glorious day when we are in reality joined in union with Him in marriage!

CD OFFER

Teaching on *Preparing the Bride of Christ* is available on CD in the United States at thirty-two dollars per set (plus six dollars shipping and handling). There are four classes on six CDs. The total cost with shipping and handling is thirty-eight dollars.

Request CDs through the e-mail address below. You will receive an e-mail through PayPal with credit card information enclosed. Please direct your request for CDs to the following e-mail address: asdelpercio@yahoo.com.